Children
AND
PARENTS

MOST REVEREND FULTON J. SHEEN

SIMON AND SCHUSTER
NEW YORK

FIRST PRINTING

SBN 671-20675-3
Library of Congress Catalog Card Number: 77-130490
Designed by Carl Weiss Associates
Manufactured in the United States of America

Acknowledgment is made to the following for permission to reprint copyrighted material:

"Yonder See the Morning Blink," from *The Collected Poems of A. E. Housman,* copyright 1922 by Holt, Rinehart & Winston, Inc.; copyright 1950 by Barclays Bank Ltd. Reprinted by permission of Holt, Rinehart & Winston, Inc.

"The Parent," from *Verses from 1929 On* by Ogden Nash, copyright 1933 by Ogden Nash. By permission of Little, Brown and Company.

Contents

Preface

A young teenager who has trouble discovering his identity is very much like a fish stranded on top of the Empire State Building. Lack of identity is emptiness—a boredom that comes from being out of an environment which gives meaning to existence—water for a fish, or a home for a child. It used to be that an abnormal person, sometimes labeled the "town fool," was protected and loved by the sanity of his neighbors. But when the milieu or the culture itself is more complex, there are no defenses to prevent loss of identity or to act as a therapy when the loss occurs. Unripe wheat pulled from the earth perishes. Youth must have some roots if it is ever to ripen into sanity.

Why does sex occupy so much of the teenager's attention? For one reason, he is not taught the goals and the purposes of life. Lacking a mission in life, he tries to make up for its absence by pursuing the intensity of sensation. A love of speeding is not so much the desire to "get there," as a way of killing the boredom of the moment. Sex concentrates on the experience, not on the purpose. Some psychiatrists give another explanation. In Victorian days, sex was repressed. Now death is repressed. Death must never be talked about to children. As Dr. Rollo May put it, "Sex is the easiest way to prove our vitality, to demonstrate we are still young, attractive and virile; to prove we are not dead yet."

Americans have the longest adolescence in the world.

Children in other countries mature much faster and get down to the serious business of living much earlier. The greater the pressures—either physical, such as the search for bread, or moral, such as the necessity to measure up to a standard—the more they will develop responsible freedom. Teenage in the United States is more cultural than biological. This is due not so much to a generation gap as to an economic condition. Being economically dependent, teenagers do not experience the hard reality of life known to parents. Even affluent men of thirty-five and fifty try to prove their juvenility by imitating the hair styles, dress and customs of the young. It is not physiology as much as the lack of responsibility which prolongs adolescence. We have all seen how quickly youths mature when they are forced to work hard either to become educated or to survive while being educated.

A key to the potential development of a teenager is to see how much he values himself. Does his sense of worth come from within, or without? Does he constantly demand approval? Does disapproval drive him into a tailspin? If so, he identifies being somebody with appearance. Extreme conformism is a sign of weakness. This imitation of others can be very serious because no one can really love others unless he loves himself and has a sense of his own personal worth. Hence the Divine Law: "Love your neighbor as you love yourself." Self-esteem begets esteem for neighbor.

One of the most serious threats to the relationship between parent and child is permissiveness. Some parents believe that if they do not give their children everything they want, the children will not love them. This may be true for any given moment, but it is not true for life. Eventually children come to despise parents who lacked character and who allowed them to grow up thinking that the world owes them a living. Having every whim satisfied while young, they could never imagine a world which would not bow down to their tantrums. Later on in life this develops into neurosis because they were never taught limitations. When these children played games, they had limitations: foul lines, umpires, referees, backfield in motion, traveling with the ball, error and managers. When they got home, there were no foul lines. They could manipulate their parents to suit their fancies and feelings. Why can't reality be that way? they asked. But it is not. Consequently, a contradiction arose between the home and the world, between the way one grows up in a family and the adult world surrounding the family.

To escape the neurosis caused by a failure to accept limitations, children sometimes become violent and aggressive in a vain attempt to make society give them what they want. It is sometimes called "the search for freedom," but it is a freedom which means the "right to do whatever I please." The secret of happy relations between parent and child is the recognition of limitations. We can draw triangles only if we give them three sides. "The Truth will make you free."

MOST REVEREND FULTON J. SHEEN, D.D., PH.D.

Love and Freedom

❧ Parents make the greatest mistake of their lives when they equate freedom with love in dealing with their children, or when they say: "But if I did not let Johnny do whatever he wanted, I would be wanting in love." Or, "Why should I teach him any morals or religion; wait until he is old enough to decide for himself." But, by the same logic, why should parents ever teach their children English? Why not wait until they are twenty-one and then let them decide which language they want to learn? Why impose habits of cleanliness, politeness or honesty? All parents who exempt themselves from exercising intelligent control and discipline over their children are social nuisances long before their children become delinquents.

What a vast Sahara separates the Western world in which freedom is identified with sentimentalism, from the Communist world where freedom is identified with tyranny. In one instance there is liberty without law, and in the other, law without liberty. Only those with character can understand the basic truth that love involves freedom, but not all freedom involves love.

Love wants to be free, but for a purpose. For example, a young man wishes to be free from parental control at a certain age in order to marry. He wants to be free from home in order to establish a home; he wants to break certain parental chains in order to forge nuptial chains which he equates with happiness. Love uses freedom to submit itself to another or for a high purpose and service. The man who loves a woman may say that he wants to be her "slave" for the rest of his life, but that kind of slavery he tells her will be his veriest liberty. No one ever falls in love without committing himself, or even subjecting himself to a purpose or a vocation. He wants to be free *from* something in order to be free *for* something.

To be entirely free in the sense of having no bonds or obligations to others would be condemning oneself to isolation. No child in a school is more lonely than the one who wants his own way in everything, and thereby finds himself shunned by those who would have been his friends. The egotist who identifies freedom with doing whatever he wants, when he wants and however he wants, may claim that he has friends, but analysis would reveal that they are merely contemporaries who are afraid to cross his will. Those in authority are not always loved. Divine Wisdom did not confer authority on Peter until he had made a triple affirmation of love.

The same love that demands freedom in order that one may submit himself to a noble cause or person, also curbs and restricts freedom. This is the side of freedom which the sentimentalists forget. Love, first of all, imposes restrictions on its own freedom. To us, many things are lawful but all are not expedient. The unspoken rebuke, the unrevealed wound, the kind word for the rapier's thrust, are limitations imposed on one's own liberty for the sake of peace and harmony. Parents reasonably restrict and limit the freedom of children for the sake of their characters, such as not giving shotguns to fifteen-year-old boys. The parent who identifies love with the feeling of love and allows a child's liberty to degenerate into license, has really only a counterfeit or neurotic love. Such emotionalism is like that of the Lady Bountiful who loves to give dances for the benefit of lepers in Nigeria, not just because the lepers need sulfone, but because it gives her the subjective pleasure of seeing herself ministering to others.

Love is not subjective, but objective; it is nourished not on fear of being unloved by one who does not get what he wants, but rather by a desire to encourage that person to develop himself to the highest reaches of his personality. No bank robber loves a policeman because he allows him to rob a bank. Nor is there a more pernicious form of optimism than to think that God is on the side of every emotional and erotic urge. Dogs love those masters best who give them commands. If children today grow up without a love for their parents, it may well be because the parents understood neither the meaning of love nor the freedom of children.

Falling in Love

◆§ Parents are lovers before they are parents. Children are the fruit of that love. Deep love tends to an enfleshment or an incarnation of others. Even God's love does this. The child is the flowering of a mutual love of husband and wife. Later comes a moment when the parents must tell their children about love, and this is not easy. It is far easier to dissect a butterfly than to tell how it flies. Deep love itself is wordless: "Would that I could utter the thoughts that arise within me." To try and put into cold words the experience of two burning flames which in turn light a torch, brings the participants to the very brink of mystery.

So deeply ingrained is this worldlessness connected with deep ecstatic love, that married life rarely speaks of it. This is fitting, for love is so delicate that it must be discovered by each new couple afresh. Words and books can explain the physiology and the biology of sex, but there are no words to express deep love except a sigh. That is why the Love of God is described in terms of "breath" or sigh—the Holy Spirit. The children understand this love best when they see the kindly esteem and affection which their parents bring to one another in the daily routine of life.

What makes telling children about sex difficult is that the word "love" has become besmirched by overusage. It used to be said: "What sins are committed in thy name, O Liberty." Now it is: "What sins are committed in thy name, O Love." Once love becomes identified with an emotional reaction or a "thrill," there is apt to be a confusion between loving a person and loving an experience. In the latter case, the person is not loved.

Girls, especially, because they are naturally more romantic, often change their sense of values within a few years. In many cases, the boy whom a girl marries at eighteen is not always the young man she would marry at twenty-one; and sometimes the one she marries at twenty-one is not the one she would marry at twenty-three. Young love either in boy or girl is often an idealization of his long hair, his ability to play a guitar, or his blond hair and blue eyes. The assumption behind this kind of love is that the girl must be as noble as she is beautiful, and that the boy must be as noble as his ability to dance.

Because love is like wine and needs time to mature, youth should not rush into marriage on the grounds that love is a sweet dream. If courtship is a dream, marriage may turn out to be an alarm clock.

Every man is incomplete; every woman is incomplete. But two incomplete things never make a perfect thing, any more than half an apple and half an onion make an applonion. Man is more incomplete than woman, because man seeks wealth and power which are both outside the woman. Marriage then is the work of two imperfect craftsmen building their dreamhouse together. They hammer their discords into harmony and mend their breaks with mercy. Then it becomes a love which never diminishes the delicacy of a woman and always increases the consideration of a man.

Freedom and the Child

❧ He who gives freedom takes a risk, but it must be taken. God foresaw the risk of making man free and planned redemption from the slavery of sin. Parents, too, run a risk when they give their children liberty.

There are two extreme errors, one of too little freedom, the other of too much. One would dam up the river, the other would destroy its banks and make a swamp.

There are also the two extremes of "Don't you do it" and "I don't care." Life for some children is one perpetual "Don't." A child of five was kept in during a storm; his mother was sewing as she chatted with a friend. "Don't do that, Freddy," she said as the child beat a tattoo on a carpet with his feet. He stopped his feet, then he began thumping his fingers. "Don't make a noise, Freddy." The boy turned to the window and then began drawing pictures on the windowpane. "Don't mark that window," was followed by "Don't go into the hall," as Freddy was looking for some way to escape from the "Don't." The little boy with a resigned air remained perfectly still for a moment and then, with a long, drawn-out sigh, he said, "Mom, is there anything that I *can* do?"

The other extreme is the "Do whatever you please" attitude. A child who always played games that had rules and "out of bounds," began to hate life that was so capricious. He finally complained to his mother, "Must I always do what I want to?"

A father who was listening to the mother read a psychology book which allowed unrestrained freedom, said to her, "Where does it say we are to apply that free hand we are supposed to have?"

Too often freedom is regarded as a source of all indiscipline. Repressive measures then are resorted to, which create fuel for rebellion. St. Augustine recalled the bitterness of his first days of school. He wrote: "I would prefer death rather than to be a child again."

Liberty often permits indiscipline, but it does not cause it. Liberty is merely a condition, and out of it may come slavery or self-government. Liberty is the condition both of obedience and of disobedience.

Liberty manifests itself sometimes in sheer negation on the part of the child and sometimes by bare affirmation. To destroy this liberty under pretext of order is to destroy the child. Nothing inferiorizes the child more than brutal imposition or constraint which prevents the unfolding of personality.

The education of liberty in a child must possess two qualities: first, it must be gradual; second, it must be associated with the moral order. It must appeal to the conscience of the educator and also to the one who is educated.

There should be a gradual unfolding of liberty according to the age of the child. In infancy, this liberty is developed sometimes by sheer imitation or by suggestion which prompts the child to act spontaneously—or as if he did not feel that any order was being given.

The peak of moral authority is reflected in the attitude of the parent who says: "I ask for obedience, because I am responsible before God for you." The child in his turn, if morally educated, will have in his heart the sentiment: "I will obey my parents because they take the place of God in my home." Where there is love, there is obedience; where there is obedience, there is the discovery of the secrets of happiness, as the scientist, by obeying the laws of nature, learns more of their secrets.

The Duties of Children to Parents

⊷§ Some learn what is right only by having their fingers burned. Psychologists who thought that children should never be restrained and be permitted to do whatever they wanted to do, have learned the folly of their theories by the heavy harvest of juvenile delinquents. From the beginning they misunderstood the mentality of children who are not happy when they are left undisciplined and undirected, for children love to be under guidance and direction. They may often test the limits of their liberty and sometimes chafe under the necessity of having their license restrained, but as dogs want a master, so children want parents who guide them.

Obedience is the law of the universe and without it the stars and the planets would fall in chaos and anarchy. The scientist learns the laws of nature only by obedience; he must sit patiently at the feet of Mother Nature and watch attentively all her actions. Once he begins to dictate how nature should operate, he shuts the door of wisdom in his face. The more passive the scientist is before the heavens, the more quickly the heavens tell the story of their fiery encampment in the skies.

St. Paul in a few sentences once gave the true relationship between parents and children. To children he wrote, "You who are children must show obedience in the Lord to your parents; it is your duty—Honor thy father and thy mother—that is the first commandment which has a promise attached to it. So it shall go well with thee, and thou shalt live long to enjoy the land." It is to be carefully noted that all arbitrary commands on the part of the parents fall outside the scope of this advice; the children are not bound to obey every whim and fancy. There is a limitation imposed for their sake, namely, "in the Lord." The parents can claim obedience because they themselves are under obedience to the Lord; authority does not start with them; it channels through them. They are not the source of law any more than Pilate who was told that he would have no authority if it did not come to him from above.

Parents in giving commands have this thought in mind: "I ask obedience of you because I am obedient to the Lord and responsible to Him." Then the children will understand that in obeying their parents they are obeying the Lord. The reason parents complain "I cannot do a thing with them" is because they never do a thing with themselves. One cannot expect the second floor of a building to stand if one pulls out the first floor; neither can we expect children to respect their parents when their parents do not respect the God who gave them their children.

A young boy who would climb into a boat and say, "I am starting off for New Zealand," would be restrained by his elders—it is to be hoped. But there would be less fear if he were placed on a ship with a good and wise captain to guide him. Parents, to some extent, are like captains of ocean liners: they know all storms and winds and currents, know where to anchor and what pitfalls to avoid. But it is not their experience which gives them authority over their children; it is rather that, as windows transmit the light of the sun, so they communicate to their children their own obedience to the Lord.

Juvenile delinquency may be corrected in this or that individual, but the root of it is beyond the children themselves. Every child is given to the parents by God as so much wax or clay to be molded into the image and resemblance of Life and Truth and Love. If the parents take their eyes off the Model, the image will become imperfect. Only those who have learned how to obey know how to command. As the dispensing of money should never be given to anyone who has not worked hard to earn it, so neither should the dispensing of authority be given to him who has not served in the ranks. If the parents themselves are like pendulums separated from the clock because they have uprooted themselves from obedience to the Divine, how shall they, with justice, tell the children that they must honor their elders? When the big wheel breaks off the axle all the little gears cease to work. The disobedience of children increases in direct proportion to the parents' decline of honor to the God above them.

The Duties of Parents to Children

⋅ჟ A young man sentenced to be electrocuted was visited by his parents in his cell. He said to them, "If it had not been for you, I should never be here." The father, speaking for the mother also, answered, "But we never told you to do any harm." "No," he rejoined, "but you never told me to do any good." The child that is allowed to do anything he pleases will eventually identify good with whatever he wants to do—whether it be stealing or raping. It was no wonder that Plato, seeing a child do some serious mischief, went and reprimanded the father for it.

But, the other side of the problem is, what is to be the attitude of parents to their children? St. Paul tells them: "You who are fathers, do not rouse your children to resentment; the training, the disciplines in which you bring them up must come from the Lord." Parents can irritate and provoke children, which is the opposite of being too soft and indifferent to their wrongdoings.

The Chinese have a proverb that says when a son is born into a family, a bow and arrow are hung before the gate. The Psalmist used the same analogy: "Children are like arrows in a warrior's hand. Happy whose quiver is well filled with these; their cause will not be set aside when they plead against their enemies at the gate." Kahlil Gibran in his beautiful poem on children says:

> You are the bows from which your children as living arrows are sent forth.
> The archer sees the mark upon the path of the infinite, and He bends you with His might that His arrows may go swift and far.
> Let your bending in the archer's hand be for gladness;
> For even as He loves the arrow that flies, so He loves also the bow that is stable.

The parent who holds the bow must be careful not to abuse and rankle the arrow. Discipline and authority are not the same as exasperating and frustrating severity. Provoking a child may gain a sullen submission, but the child himself is smart enough to know of the injustice. Parents can incite resentment in children in several ways: one is by giving too many commands, with the result that the child hears none. A magazine once compiled a list of some of the directions which children never hear; one of them was: "Kiss your Aunt Lucy." When the requirement is more than can be reasonably rendered, it becomes an annoyance and a vexation. Another way to make children think less of their parents is to continually blame the children for the wrong they have done, or else give all commandments in terms of "Don't." To condemn when there is no sure ground for complaint is to sting the child with injustice.

The child who is never encouraged or praised when he does well, but always criticized when he does wrong, is apt to feel there is no reason for doing the things that are good except to avoid a scolding.

Correction and submission are to be given in the spirit of the Lord. Parents who know themselves to be disciples of the Lord know best how to make disciples of their own children. Children are much more sensitive than is generally believed; their growing sense of self-respect does not like to be wounded; parents who roar and shout at children and reiterate their faults and foibles, keep opening wounds which the children themselves are trying to close and forget. A balance must, therefore, be struck between the kindness of the parents and the obedience of children. If no discipline or obedience is expected of children, they will grow up suffering a moral loss which life can never remedy. Parents who selfishly grant every whim of their children later on will feel the barbed agony of their children's selfishness. Parents should be like shepherds who lead their sheep as the Lord walked before His disciples, showing them the way. Then there will never be an abuse of power. If the Lord does not teach, guide and nourish the child, the devil will. Youth is for learning, manhood is for acting and old age is for enjoying the fruits of both. The parent is the best teacher who has God as his teacher.

Love in the Family

✎§ Families are on the move. A little over a hundred years ago, about sixty-five percent of the population of the country lived on farms; presently, the figure is about twelve percent. About one-fifth of pregnant women continue to work during the pregnancy. Almost half the women who have been married from six to ten years are working, thus creating the problem of caring for the children during the day.

It used to be that the family made the church—the parish being the sum of families. Today it is the church which makes the family; keeps them together, helps educate the children while parents are at work, and prepares the young for marriage. Throughout the Old Testament, the home was the center of virtue and culture. In the New Testament, many a youth was instructed to return to his home after being delivered from evil, such as the young man from the land of the Gerasenes—the prodigal returns home. The Lord visits the home of a dishonest tax collector and has a meal with his peers; He joins in a marriage feast in one home, and grieves with the father who has lost a daughter. But all the while He is without a home. "The foxes have their holes, the birds of the air their nests, but the Son of Man has nowhere to lay His head."

What is the family? The family is a place where two mysteries are enacted: first, it is the area where the unlovable are loved, and second, it is the environment in which love solves personality problems.

We do not say that it is wholly a place of love, because there are tensions in the home as well as anywhere else. As Ogden Nash wrote:

Children won't be happy with nothing to ignore
So that's what parents were created for.

There is no merit in loving others who are lovable. It is easy to love lovable children, but to love them when they are unlovable is the unfailing sign of a family. One mother gave a party for the children of the neighborhood. Ice-cream cones were brought to each child. Her child began screaming, "This is vanilla; I don't want vanilla." The mother answered, "Listen, I didn't want you either; but now that I have you, I have learned to love you. You love that va-

nilla." When children are cantankerous, rebellious and
shriek their heads off, particularly on rainy days, it is very
difficult to love them with patience. But once parents recognize that God loves them even when they are unlovable,
it inspires them to do the same for their children.

Curious it is how one can love and hate at the same time;
but we do. How can I love God and still sin? St. Paul said,
"The good I will to do, I do not; and the evil I will not,
that I do." This contrariety of emotions at one and the
same time does not prove love is not primary in our
makeup. Parents love the children through their squab-
bles, tantrums and furies, and so God loves us through
ours. As He puts love where He does not find it, so parents
put love where they do not find, for the moment, anything
lovable; but thus they become lovable.

The second mark of the true family spirit is to use love
to solve personality problems. The tragedy of our day is
that so many are unloved; they are used, but they are not
loved. How often friends are made on this basis: "They can
get it wholesale." But in a family love makes children normal. Frederick II of the thirteenth century brought together a number of abandoned children and put them in
the care of nurses, who were instructed never to speak a
word to the children, nor show any facial emotion or ges-
ture of love. Frederick wanted to find out what language
they would speak. The experiment failed. All the children
died, and they died for want of love.

A similar experiment was made with monkeys. The
young ones were taken away from their mothers; half of
them were allowed to go near an imitation monkey that
was electrically heated, and could also simulate an embrace. The other little monkeys had no monkey-mother,
real or artificial. The first monkeys grew up to be like
other monkeys, but those who lacked even simulated affection grew to be the "craziest monkeys." In the London
Blitz, some children were removed from London to the

country; others were left with mothers in the bombardment. The children who were with mothers in the Blitz were in better health than those who were evacuated, though they spent their time with other people.

The family then is a place where, under the influence of love, we learn from mistakes rather than a place where we are punished for them. Discipline, however, is not to be disowned. Nothing develops character like a pat on the back, provided it is given hard enough, often enough and low enough. Only he who loves, may punish.

Just Discipline

◄§ The practices of bygone times have interest for all of us. One custom now out of date and forgotten is spanking. It is well to remember that every newborn child gets a spanking to start him breathing and living. For the benefit of those who do not know of the phenomenon called "spanking" it might be called a form of punishment that is given at one end to impress the other.

There are psychological reasons for the decline of spanking. It is argued that any form of physical discipline of a child overpowers him physically; and to overpower a child physically or mentally is bad for him, for it crushes his ego. It is false to suggest that to overpower a child in any way whatsoever is wrong. A music teacher overpowers a boy when he starts giving him trumpet lessons. A boxer overpowers a novice in teaching pugilism. Every doctor overpowers a patient in injecting a needle. It is curious that they who are opposed to control over youth, are tolerant of teenagers who take dope which so completely overwhelms their character and their intelligence.

A child psychologist was once defined as "one who will never strike a child, except in self defense." Anyone who is old enough to remember being spanked will recall that waiting for it is worse than the spanking itself. No threat in all the world so takes on the appearance of a black cyclonic cloud as telling a child: "Wait until your father gets home." A child once said, "I would rather be spanked than talked to." Another said, "Spanking does not last long. It shows who is boss."

One other objection that has been made against spanking is that afterward parents feel ashamed or guilty. This is true when the punishment is excessive, emotional, out of all proportion to the offense, or given arbitrarily. It should be pointed out, however, that these same people are not ashamed when they scold a servant, howl at a husband or growl at the butcher who overcharged them a few cents. One parent said to a child, "This hurts me more than it does you." The child answered, "Yes, but not in the same place."

Parents hold authority from God over their children and are responsible for them. Their children are as so much clay in their hands and what they become later on depends upon the way they have been molded. The authority given to the parents does not exist for their good, but for the good of those under them, just as the authority given to a pilot on a plane is not just for himself, but for the good of his passengers.

This is not a plea for the restoration of spanking, but rather to affirm respect for parental authority which once used that method of making actions speak louder than words. It is not true to say that there is in general a reaction against parental authority; it is more truthful to say that the parents have lacked those qualities which command respect, particularly a want of moral values. A father or mother on a second or third marriage naturally has great

difficulty in convincing a child to "never break your word."
The respect that one has for a rule flows naturally from the
respect that one has for the person who gives it. If Mickey
Mantle gave a suggestion to a boy about how to hold a bat,
there would be an immediate bending of energy to conform to that precept.

Every defect in character creates a defect in obedience.
Three out of five delinquents come from homes where
there is discord between parents. Seven out of ten delinquents come from broken homes where there is no family
life. Whether it be a general in an army, a bishop in a diocese, a teacher in a school or a parent in a home, there will
never be a respect for a command unless there is respect for
the commander. It is earnestly to be hoped that the youngsters who are growing up now will not so much say, "The
last generation has failed me," but rather, "I will not fail
the next generation."

Spanking

◆⋄ If the word "spanking" may be used as a symbol of any
kind of discipline, it is safe to say that there is a direct ratio
between juvenile delinquency and lack of discipline in the
home. Putting it more lightly: factors contributing to juvenile delinquency have been safety razors which have dis-
pensed with the razor strap, and garages which have done
away with the woodshed. To borrow shipboard terminol-
ogy, spanking is known as "stern" punishment. It is a form
of depressing one end to impress the other end. It takes
much less time than reasoning and penetrates more quickly
to the seat of wisdom. There almost seems to be providen-
tial order between a parent and a child. God gave parents a
hand, and he also gave the child an extremely well-padded

part of his anatomy; one was made for the other in extreme cases.

A former headmaster of Philips Andover Academy said, "I was whipped as a child, thank goodness. Time and time again I had to throw boys out of the school, and all they needed was a good spanking."

The Divine word of God in Scripture is certainly not opposed to discipline on the part of the parent, but rather recommends it. The Book of Proverbs states, "A rod for the back of him who is devoid of understanding." And again, "He that spareth the rod, hateth his son; but he that loves him chasteneth him betimes." Scripture does not seem to anticipate any evil effects from spanking, "Withhold not correction from the child, for if thou beatest him with a rod, he shall not die." Later on we read, "Chasten the son while there is hope, and let not thy soul spare for his crying."

A child psychologist who had written much against spanking saying that it was "cruel" was arrested for locking his crying children in the car for eight hours while he and his wife went to the theater and to dinner. One is not to fear evil results because the child is overpowered. Every child is intellectually overpowered by his teacher inasmuch as there is the superiority of truth.

If parents say they feel ashamed after punishing a child, this is because their discipline may have been excessive or out of all proportion to the offense. These same people are not the least bit ashamed when they reprimand a cook.

If it be said that spanking is the expression of the system, let it be admitted that it is not an expression of authoritarianism, but authority. It is to be noted that in the commandments of God, the first three express our duties to God. The last six commandments are duties to our neighbors. In between is the fourth commandment, which is the duty that is owed to parents by children. The very order of the commandments indicates that God intended the parents to take His place in the home; the obedience which is due them is the reflection of the obedience which is due to God Himself.

There is nothing that develops character like a pat on the back, provided that it is given often enough, hard enough and low enough. Spanking is one of the most easily understood lessons in the world. It requires no explanation; no fine points are involved. It is quick, clean-cut, clears the air, allows no long periods of disfavor and helps the parent by preventing an accumulation of emotional worries.

Two Kinds of Discipline

ε§ The higher one rises in nature, the greater is the adaptability to change. The higher we rise in the scale of life, the wider is the scope and possibility of training. For example, water is capable of being only three forms—ice, liquid and steam. The dog or the elephant is capable of a greater variety of training than the snail or the butterfly. Because man is endowed with intelligence, he is capable of choosing his own goals which animals cannot do, for they have their purposes imposed upon them by instinct. Granted this great variety of purposes, the human being is capable of being trained. The range of his possible training is practically unlimited. One never asks a little pig what kind of a hog he is going to be when he grows up; but one does ask a child what manner of man or woman he or she will be. They are, under their parents, little creators of their destiny—even the eternal one.

Discipline or training is of two kinds—one external, which has to do with the rule, and the other internal, which has to do with reason and conscience. Both are re-

lated to obedience. Interior discipline does not so much
look to a rule, but to the values which inspired it. It is
based upon the fact that everyone is a possible saint.

To tell children that they are lazy or worthless, develops
in them a sense of inferiority. In an adult, this sometimes
makes a person put forth efforts to overcome the failure,
but the extreme sensibility of a child does not cause that
kind of reaction. To tell a child that he is a thief may cause
thievery to increase, unless some cure is administered.
Children are apt to take the decision of adults passively. It
is a great mistake to limit education to the simple observation of a defect; it is sterile and does no good.

A psychologist once said, "At the bottom of all vices,
there is a condemnation in which one does believe." It is
not wrong to bring out a defect provided one offers a cure.
One should never dig a hole unless something is put into it.
The psychologist should have changed his statement to the
effect that at the base of all virtues, there is a value in
which one does believe.

The sense of inferiority is increased when the correction
of a child is humiliating; no sanction is worthwhile unless
it does good to the child. Every humiliation always brings
a defense, hence there should not be a correction without
some enlightenment of conscience. A sense of inferiority
can also have several bad reactions, such as pride, melan-
choly and laziness.

Severity is primarily an exaggeration of the distance between child and parent, or anyone who holds the position
of the parent. It is also a lack of regard for the individual
nature of the child. Authority exists for the sake of those
over whom it is set, not for its own sake. The military salute is not accorded to the personality of the general, but to
his rank.

Excessive authority always originates in a false concept of
authority. Such parents think they exercise authority for
the good of the child, whereas the source of it is an overesti-

mation of their own ego. The leader who is sure of his position does not need to make extreme demonstrations of authority.

The greatest authority over the child is the mastery of oneself on the part of the parent. When the child discovers in the parent no passion and no weakness that he can use, he feels himself incapable of destroying the parents. Their tenderness and sweetness will have for him then the value which inspires respect. The child, on the other hand, who is able to communicate his wrath and his impatience to his parents, will soon exchange respect for his own force.

Every child is like a mirror in the sense that he reflects the influences that are around him and transforms them into his own nature. Hence, the first principle of education is to educate oneself and to be a model.

Obedience

 हुई Obedience is an act of accord between a rule of reason and the will to submit. True obedience does not exist in early infancy, because it demands intellectual and moral capacities which have not yet evolved in the child.

Up until the age of reason, the child does not really obey. He is subject to an ensemble of rules and regulations such as when he will go to bed, the clothes he will wear, where he will put his toys. The obedience here is passive; it is associated with praise and blame, and also an instinctive reverence for his parents. There is, however, something sacred about the commands of adult origin, and this sacredness varies with the moral worth of the parents. The child is quicker in making moral judgments about his elders than is generally admitted. This is the age where mechanism of obedience is developed which saves the child from

capricious action. Habits of virtue are inculcated before
there is a knowledge of the reason of virtue, just as a child
is taught cleanliness before knowing the reason for it. It is
only, therefore, a provisory basis on which true obedience
is found.

Obedience in a child varies from age to age, as there is
progress toward self-government. From the age of seven to
thirteen, the child is stripped progressively of his egocentrism. In school, he is in contact with other personalities and there is awakened in him the exigencies of a social
order. At this point, conscience is developed which requires the necessity of rule. Sometimes the rule seems opposed to his own; he may submit to it through an inner
sentiment of fear, respect, affection or obedience. If pre-
sented properly, the obedience becomes positive, the submission becomes acceptation. All obedience demands some
kind of effort and there must be attached to it, therefore,
some interest which will favor the one who obeys. A for-
mula such as "do this and you will please me" is much
more effective than the injunction "do this." Also helpful
is the appeal "do this and you will be a man." The appeal to
victory strongly interests the child from seven to thirteen.

With puberty, a new crisis of growth produces a drive for
independence which very often asserts itself against the
constraint of the adult. Here there is a kind of oscillation
between the desire to choose freely and the desire to be
counseled which will put an end to decision. The curve of
obedience, however, shows great progress when the authority is someone who is well liked. Experiments have shown
that the adolescent loves firmness and he will attach himself to an energetic and intelligent chief. As Paul Tournier,
one of the great psychologists, put it, "There is no kind of
superiority which does not excite their enthusiasm."

The desire for independence on the one hand and the
desire for order on the other, are both manifestations of the
unfolding of personality. This oscillation between obedi-

ence and disobedience is merely the concave and convex sides of the saucer. It is hard to see both together, as it is difficult to see the Matterhorn from the Swiss side and the Italian side at the same time, though we know they are aspects of the same reality. The child wants dependence and he wants independence. The secret is for the parent to see them under different relations. So far as the youth is concerned, he wants an absence of responsibility; as far as others are concerned, the youth wants total responsibility. It is the parents themselves who make this distinction. When they are outraged at what a neighbor does to them, they hold the neighbor blameworthy; but when the neighbor accuses them of the same misconduct, they find excuses. The reconciliation of the tension in the child between obedience and disobedience can be accomplished by training him to make his obedience internal instead of external; to make him see himself responsible not only in the face of his parents but in relation to others. It is not rules which irritate the child; it is rules without reason. He plays his games according to rules. He just wants to have some part in either the making or application of the rules. Thus he will come to see reason and responsibility behind the laws.

Should Parents Obey Children?

◆§ If one accepted uncritically some of the educational and psychological theories current in the world, the answer to the above would have to be in the affirmative. On the basis of such false ideas, educators and juvenile delinquents would support the thesis that parents should never exercise authority over their children, but rather obey the children in all things. The Fourth Commandment would then read:

"Father and Mother, obey thy children." Some would argue that parents should obey children because:

1. If they do not, their children will never love them when they grow up. To love means to give pleasure; and to refuse to give pleasure is not to be loved. Parents who do not give children what they like will be penalized later on in life by being unliked.

2. If the parents do not obey the child, but rather insist on obedience, the child will develop a guilt-complex, and every guilt-complex is abnormal. If parents insist when a boy has stolen a bicycle that: *"Thou shalt not steal,"* or, "You pay back what you have stolen," the boy will thereby develop a taboo, a superego and an inhibition which will ruin his future life. Later on he will be obliged to go to a psychoanalyst to get rid of the guilt-complex.

3. By insisting on obedience, parents would thereby destroy the freedom of the child. To be free means to do whatever you please. Every command is a restraint of liberty. To demand of the child that he tell you whether or not he joined a gang and stole an automobile, without giving him the right to invoke the Fifth Amendment in answer to your question, is a violation and a destruction of the basic liberties guaranteed by the Constitution of this great country.

4. If parents do not obey their children, but insist on being obeyed, they will thereby become authoritarian, and what has caused all the political mischief in the world if it be not authoritarianism?

5. Commands will develop an inferiority complex in the child. Nothing more quickly inferiorizes the child than to be obliged to look up to his parents as superior to himself. A noted educator put it this way: "Why should my children obey me because I have a few gray hairs on my head?" It is superior beings and not inferior beings which make the world. The ego was meant to be developed and unfolded,

not to be curtailed; self-expression is always right and self-repression is always wrong.

Unfortunately, some refutation of these false assumptions is necessary:

1. Love of children for parents does not depend on whether they give way to every wish of the child, but whether the parents possess those moral qualities which command respect and love.

2. To call every act of wrongdoing the potential source of a "guilt-complex" and to make it abnormal is to deny that we are responsible for our misdeeds. But to deny responsibility is to deny freedom.

3. Freedom does not mean the right to do whatever you please, but the right to do whatever you ought. Freedom is related to law and truth. "The truth will make you free." Freedom to do whatever you please is a physical, not a moral right. It is identical with license and anarchy, which in turn, by reaction, creates Communism or the right to do whatever you must. Communism is the forcible organization of chaos created by false liberty or license.

4. Authoritarianism may be based either on force or on love. When there is love, there is no feeling that authority is imposed. The man who loves a woman gives her gifts, but under no constraint, except the constraint of affection. Because I love the authority of Christ in the Church, I never feel under constraint, but I do feel the pull and the thrill of love.

5. What is so wrong about developing a sense of inferiority? When everyone is a little god, then war starts between the conflicting egotists. John the Baptist, when he saw Our Lord coming, said, "I must decrease; He must increase." Pride brings ruin; the more the ego becomes filled with self, the more quickly it sinks. It still is true that children should honor their father and their mother.

The Importance of Habits

ఴ Disobedience in a child is inspired by different motives at different ages. The disobedience of a child between the ages of three and four is very often nothing else but the consciousness of his own ego up against other egos. The child is merely discovering his own existence, and one of the ways he does this is by a kind of revolt. Having passed through a period when he got whatever he wanted by crying, he never thought of other people as having rights. Completely locked in egocentricity, he did not see any reason for giving way to the rules of others. The hard knocks of other children at school, where he is forced to correct his own illusions of egocentrism, is one way to overcome this kind of disobedience.

Disobedience at a later stage, from seven to twelve, is a more authentic disobedience, both against external orders and constraint. Often at this time he feels the pressure of rules to which he is bound to submit. Interest plays the same role at this age that egocentrism played in the first stage of disobedience. He obeys when it is to his interest or advantage; he disobeys when it is not to his interest. Parents often commit the fallacy of believing that the child will develop a complex if he is asked to do what he does not want to do. No child would ever be housebroken if this idea were carried through.

The parent who believes in allowing the child to do what he pleases, does so under the false pretext of respecting the liberty of the child. But the child is as yet incapable of good self-government. Only a fully developed being is capable of autonomy. The child only comes to it progressively. There is first the acceptance of the rule; later on comes an interior adhesion to the rule, which is the true sign of liberty and is expressed by obedience. Obedience habituates the child to forget immediate desires for the sake of higher duties.

Some parents know they are incapable of demanding obedience, so they capitulate before disobedience. Lacking moral worth, they allow moral worthlessness. The result is that the child soon becomes the slave of his own caprices, which are much more imperious than any commands that he might have been given. A confirmed little egotist who expects everybody to do his will is eventually frustrated and ends up on the psychoanalytic couch.

Affection and tenderness, which are essential, lose their happy effect if they degenerate into indiscipline. Parents who are not wanted in the homes of their children when they are old, are evidence of the want of true affection in the children. Parents who never commanded respect, pay the penalty later on in life.

Where there is true authority, there is never any necessity of the parent having to defend his dignity; rather the parent defends the child against himself. True authority makes the child conscious of his own fault; false authority makes the parent defend himself.

Authority is an appeal to obedience or to willing adherence to a rule on the part of the child. There must be some parallel between the use of authority and the moral maturity of the child.

The exterior act of obedience precedes the virtue of obedience. The first acts of obedience compensate for deficiencies of judgment and will on the part of the child. These gradually develop in him a control over his own activity. Later on, he will use this control to judge what is right and what is wrong.

Rousseau said, "The only habit which one ought to develop in a child is the habit never to be contradicted." This is a double error: a pedagogical error, because a good habit liberates the child from caprice and prepares for the unfolding of liberty; a psychological error, for bad habits can develop without correction. What is often forgotten is the importance of habits in the training of the young. If good habits are not inculcated, evil habits will develop, and then comes juvenile delinquency when the weeds of self will overrun the roses that grow only by pruning and sacrifice.

Character

✒§ When I was a little boy my father gave me a saw. I then became a tool-using animal. The saw was an extension of my personality. But the first thing I did was to saw into the side of a wagon. "I came, I saw and I conquered."

I could not disclaim the responsibility for the damage done by this extension of my personality, because the saw was mine once I had said, "this is mine."

Another example of the extension of personality is in a boy contemplating his possessions. Coventry Patmore in his poem entitled "The Toys" describes how a little boy—his mother being dead—got into trouble with his father, was punished and sent to bed. The father then visits the son who has cried himself to sleep. To recompense for the father's seeming lack of affection, the boy has placed all his "treasures"—stones, seashells, etc.—on the table next to him "to comfort his sad heart."

The moment love was withdrawn, a compensation was found by contemplating the extension of his personality, which his shells and stones represented.

There seems to be an over-compensation for the losses to personality by acquiring things. As soon as our personality begins to be empty of love, or when we feel starved of affection, we seek to enrich ourselves on the outside.

Thus we begin to mistake what we have, for what we are. The more empty a soul is, the more it tries to fill itself on the outside. When Adam and Eve lost the inner grace they had, they made clothes for themselves. They had to compensate by external appearance for the loss of internal beauty of soul. People given to excessive luxury are those who are most naked on the inside. If man were only a material thing, then he should extend his personality by acquiring as many material possessions as possible. But if man is spiritual, then enrichment must be on the inside; not in *having*, but in *being*.

Not everyone wants this enrichment. The painting by Holman Hunt entitled "The Light of the World" in St. Paul's, London, emphasizes this. The Master is standing, holding a lantern which throws its light on a closed door. We perceive no latch on the door. There is a compassionate look upon the Master's face, who is earnestly seeking entrance. Hunt was asked why he put no latch on the outside of the door. He said that it was because the entrance is on the inside. Christ is the Lover of souls, but not the burglar of souls. "If any man will open the door to Me, I will come in and sup with him and he with Me."

A boy sometimes says, "I do not want to go to school." But his mother insists on his going. She is bent on developing the inside of her son's personality.

Our attitude toward the world is often like the boy's attitude toward school. We say, "I just want to be happy; I want to go through the world without any pain." We forget that being sent to school is a loving discipline. When the boy asked to be kept from school he was asking for less love, not more; for less motherliness, not more.

God does not let us stay away from school. Love pays such a tribute to our worth that it never spares us trial and pain and struggle by which evil is undone and good is achieved.

Courtesy

✿§ What has happened to politeness? How few children, for example, are ever trained to shake hands with a person to whom they are introduced. Mothers say, "Jimmie, put out your hand." Courtship is much more polite than marriage; as one husband said to his wife who had asked him to hand her the evening paper, "The chase is over; I have bagged the game." The automobile is almost like a shield against manners when driving on the highway. Enclosed in a steel cage and traveling at a high rate of speed, one is always anonymous to the other person, or to whom one honks the horn in rage, or gives Dirty Look No. 1864.

What are the causes for this want of delicacy and refinement toward others in modern society? One reason probably is that we live in a technological age in which we are separated from one another by functions. Persons become like fountain pens with which business organizations write; whether the ink is black, red, green or yellow makes little difference. The sense of the uniqueness of the person, his irreplaceability, his bearing of eternal values—all this is lost. If "A" does not press the button, there is always "B" who will perhaps be a better button-pusher.

It is pointless to analyze causes. Much more important is how to restore politeness in society. When we speak of courtesy we do not mean it as did Emerson when he wrote, "Manners have been somewhat cynically defined to be a contrivance of wise men to keep fools at distance." But evidently Emerson did not share this view for he held, "Life is short, but there is always time for courtesy."

Also to be outlawed from consideration is a feigned or

dissembling courtesy of which Shakespeare said, "How this fine tyrant can tickle when she wounds."

The greatest treatise on courtesy ever written was in a letter to the people of Corinth in which, among other things, the man of Tarsus wrote, "Love has good manners and does not pursue selfish advantage. It is not touchy. It does not keep account of evil or gloat over the wickedness of other people. On the contrary, it is glad with all good men when truth prevails. Love knows no limit to its endurance, no end to its trust, no fading of its hope; it can outlast everything. It is in fact, the one thing that stands when all else has fallen."

This idea has been developed by Newman in his *Idea of a University Defined*. To the above qualities of politeness, Newman added that "a gentleman or a courteous man is one who never gives pain."

Courtesy manifests itself in the trivial things of life rather than in the large donation and the great show. As a woman would rather have a thousand little courtesies and signs of affection from her husband than one burst of carnal aggressiveness, so politeness is in the trivial and the commonplace. Take, for example, the kindness of Boaz who told his reapers to purposefully leave a few sheaves of grain so that Ruth would find them. Thoughtfulness of this kind is not learned from a book of etiquette because true courtesy goes beyond the established norms of good manners. The true gentleman does more than the book requires.

Another rule of courtesy is: "In lowliness of mind, let each esteem others better than themselves." (St. Paul: Epistle to the Philippians 2:3.) This is difficult. But it is born of the Christian law that we can see the actions of people, but cannot know the motives. We always think the best about ourselves, but we think only the worst about other people, particularly today when the mood is to be rebels without programs, to pull down rather than to build up. There is always room to esteem others, because we *know* the worst about ourselves, but we can only *suspect* the worst about our fellowmen. Hence we may believe that they are really better than we are. This is the foundation of the statement attributed to so many: "There but for the grace of God go I."

Out of the Barbed Mouths of the Young

A good rule to follow when one is the object of a barbed criticism, or when one hears another vilified is: "Consider not *what* the critic says, but *why* he says it." Two young women were discussing an absent third. One thought she was pretty for she had dimples. The other retorted, "Weak face muscles." The "why" of the judgment was jealousy. As Mark Twain once said, "There's always something about your success that displeases even your best friend. He would like to be in your boots. So envy provides the mud that failure throws at success."

The above rule applies even to the conversation of children and teenagers. Though they live in a world of close personal relationships, they will come up with the most abstract questions as if they were little philosophers. One child wanted to know, "How many abandoned children are there in New York City?" The parent of course did not know, so the child followed it up with, "How many are there in the world?" If the father gave an exact statistic, it would never have satisfied. The parent should have asked himself "why" did the child ask the question? The child was interested because he overheard talk about his parents divorcing and he was afraid of being abandoned. Parents complain that they "reason with the children until blue in the face, but it does no good." They have failed to look to the motivation which prompted the inquiry.

When the young relate an event or happening, they do not do so as a newspaper reporter. The latter is concerned only with the face or the "what." The child's interest, however, is in the relationship of that event to the parent. "You gave Johnny the big piece of pie and you gave me the little one." It does no good to say that Johnny is two years old, or that the piece was not much bigger. The issue is: Do you love me as much as you love him, despite appearances? Hence the wise mother will quickly ask "why" and do two things. First, she may say, "You were wondering about my love for you, weren't you?" Second, she will hug the questioner and the famous Buber quotient of I-Thou is worked out perfectly.

Conversation with children has three sides: First, the parent must listen to what the child says; second, figure out what was behind the conversation; and finally, enter into a conversation proving that you understand it. Children's questions can very often be tricky. They are often better psychologists than the parents who take everything at its face value and ignore the feeling or the fear or the craving for sympathy which is hidden therein. "I am terrible in spelling" is a truth. Johnny does not know how to spell. The father answers an equal truth, "You sure are a lousy speller."

Then begin the hard feelings and maybe tears. The child said that he could not spell, not to have his ignorance reaffirmed; rather, he was looking for understanding and sympathy. If the father had said, "I can remember when I was in your grade; I missed three out of five words in a spelling contest. One of them was 'which' which I spelled 'witch.' But I spell correctly today, and I know you will do as well some day." To receive encouragement and assurance of faith is the reason why the child humbled himself in the first place.

Parents work on a conscious level; children on the subconscious. Parents are scientists; children are psychologists. Fathers are matter-of-fact; children are meaning-of-fact. Trying to practice a little psychology, a mother may tell her brat of a son, "You are such a good boy." He is not fooled. He knows he is being flattered in the hope of making him good. Only last week he told his mother that he wished that she would choke to death on fishbones. Perceiving the sham of the mother's praise, he begins to act worse than ever to prove his "true" self as opposed to the hoped-for-self of the mother. How often before company comes a child is praised for being so quiet and polite and respectful, but as soon as the company arrives, he begins to prove how wrong his mother really is. The mother went too far in praising him for his good behavior; hence, it ceased to be an encouragement. Detecting dishonesty in the mother, the child reacts dishonestly. She says he is good when he is not, so he will be bad to prove that she lied. Children are far wiser than we think.

Maybe we have too many books on Child Psychology and not enough on Parent Psychology. One of the most important chapters would be to teach parents "Why they say it."

Educating Children

ᴥᔥ Gilbert K. Chesterton once said, "We send our children to school too late to be educated." By this he meant that education begins early. Parents can go wrong in the early training if they hold to either one of two mistaken beliefs concerning human nature. One belief that started a few centuries ago is that an infant is intrinsically corrupt, and the other, more recent, that the infant has only good tendencies. The truth is in between the two extremes: A child is a seed of neither virtue nor vice; he has a tendency to be both bad and good.

In the face of these facts, there can be two kinds of discipline: one exterior, and the other, interior.

The external rule makes for regularity. The child is put off by the unhabitual and disconcerting; he does not understand exception. For the adult, the exception confirms the rule; for the child, it ruins him. One of the reasons why children sometimes are a little calmer in school is because the employment of time is methodical and they are less subjected to random and unpredictable changes.

The reason for an external rule is that it facilitates duties by mechanizing action through habits; it spares effort and rescues the child from the necessity of adapting himself to an entirely new situation. It is important in cleanliness, table manners and respect for visitors. It would be a grave error, however, to suppose that the rule ought to install itself in the soul in a purely extrinsic manner. It must be such as to respond to the need of the child.

The child desires nothing more than not to be a child. He selects that which will make him grow and rejects everything that will recall his weakness as a child. He will love the rule, however, if he can see that it will help him to grow and if it enables him to become a man. Exterior discipline is mechanical; the punishment follows the crime without any thought of the personality of the child. Exterior discipline looks to the social order but interior discipline looks to the soul itself. One can force someone to take a step, but one cannot force someone to be just.

In one instance there is obedience to rule and in another, obedience to conscience. Both the external rule or conformity to social standards, and internal rule or conformity to conscience, first expressed by the parent and later by the child, play their roles in educating the child.

Authority is the art of creating obedience. Obedience is not the absolute end of authority. When obedience becomes a fetish, it creates disobedience by reaction. Here there is egotism on the part of the adult who looks more to himself than the child. He is defending his own personality which would be disrupted by disobedience. The parent who overemphasizes the external rule equates authority with obedience. He who seeks obedience for itself, loses it. He sometimes gets exterior order, but never interior adhesion. Obedience is not the end of authority; it is the effect of authority. Authority does not cause obedience; it attracts it. Authority is grounded on moral prestige and value. Authority is attached to a person. That is why delegated authority is often provisory (for example, a baby sitter), because it is not animated by that moral force which is possessed by the good parent. When the one who commands is not normally good, refuge is sought either in tyranny on the part of the parent, or license on the part of the child. Authority is moral force; obedience is the sign of a strong personality, capable of freely giving himself. A slave does not obey; he is subject.

The union of authority and obedience is, therefore, the token of two values which demand one another and which ought to be an equilibrium. If the force of authority is lost, obedience loses its point of support. Juvenile delinquency increases in direct proportion to the decline of moral worth on the part of the parents.

Work and Play

ह§ When I was a boy I used to play baseball during the summer on a vacant lot nearby. Sometimes my mother would call me, "I want you to go to the grocery store to get . . ." My usual retort was, "Why can't I go later?" Her answer generally was, "What difference is there between running after groceries and running for a ball?" I never could think of an answer.

Later on when I studied philosophy I came across the brilliant answer in the writings of St. Thomas Aquinas. He argued that there is a great difference between work and play. Work is for a purpose. Play is not. Play is just for fun. There was the answer, but it came too late. Running to the store had a purpose; chasing a fly ball did not. By this time, my mother must know the answer in heaven, but I am happy that I found it—even on earth.

It is recorded of St. John the Evangelist that one of his disciples was scandalized at seeing him play. He told the narrow-minded man to take a bow and shoot the arrow into the sky. When he had done this several times, he asked him if he could keep it up all day and night, to which the answer came that the bow would break. In like manner, he said that man's mind would break if the tension of study and work were not occasionally relaxed.

Play is often associated with children in contrast to the serious-minded activites of adults. But the German writer Schiller with much more profundity held that "man only plays when in the full meaning of the word he is a man, and he is perfectly human only when he plays." The Dutch historian Johan Huizinga holds that "civilization arises and unfolds itself in play . . . genuine pure play is one of the main bases of civilization."

Play is related to work, for if every day were the Fourth of July, who would enjoy fireworks?

Cicero compared it to sleep as well as work. "It is indeed lawful to make use of play and fun, but in the same way as we have recourse to sleep and other kinds of rest, and then only when we have done our duty in grave and serious matters." Scripture compares creation to work, but, and this is rarely stated, also to play. In Proverbs, these two elements of creation are combined. First, there is the formation of the world, the giving it purpose and meaning, but linked with it is the contrasting idea of play.

> I was by His side, a Master Craftsman
> Delighting Him day after day,
> Ever at play in His Presence, at play everywhere in His
>   world,
> Delighting to be with the sons of men.

The message is about Wisdom or the Word of God before He became flesh in Christ at Bethlehem. First, there is the work of the six days in contradiction to the rest on the Sabbath. All things were made by the Power of the Word. The serious side of Divinity is like unto the seriousness of a sculptor molding clay according to the plan existing in his mind.

But why is play associated with work? Why the lightness and the delight during the labor of creation? God was not forced to labor for six phases of evolution before He could rest. No obligation ever forced love to go outside Himself. Like play, creation was not forced. God was under no obligation to project His Love into hearts and His Truth to the minds and His Being into things. While creation was full of serious purpose, it was as empty of necessity as love.

How curious that several centuries before Christ, the wise Plato in his *Timeus* speaks of the Logos or the Mind of the Universe holding, like a child, the sphere of the earth within his hands. Here, too, is the tension between Almighty Power and childlike ease. It was this notion of Plato's which so often inspired medieval artists to picture the Infant Christ as holding an apple in his hand, the symbol of the universe. Father John Banister Tabb followed this up in poetry describing how the Infant Child lost his ball, the earth, and came down to our poor human level to find it again.

What is mingled here is the serious and the light, the tragic and the comic. As Shakespeare asked in his *A Midsummer Night's Dream*, "Is there no play to ease the anguish of a torturing hour?" Cicero, so skilled in oratory, recommended this interplay of work and play, "When the audience is weary, it will be useful to the speaker to try something novel or amusing, provided that it be not incompatible with the gravity of the subject."

The lighthearted and the serious then, go together in life. "I hold," writes Xenophon, the ancient Greek, "that the works of good and lovable men are worthy of memory, not only when they have been carried out in a serious vein, but also in the spirit of play." The real man is, therefore, the grave-merry man; he knows very well that there is a place for crying and laughing; for giving purpose to his work and still lightly doing the things that are unnecessary. As Francis of Sales wrote, "A sad saint is a sorry kind of saint." Life has a serious side: We have to work out our salvation; but it is also amusing and laughable because we take ourselves so seriously in other things that are not so important.

Caring

✑§ A little girl cut her finger, which the mother bandaged and partly healed with a kiss. She ran upstairs to her father. He was busy working on income tax, just looked at her, and turned to his work. She came down crying because of the double cut. To her mother who asked the reason for the tears, she said, "He didn't even say 'oh.'"

Some of the most tragic moments in life are those when we cannot find an audience, not just for good news or for secrets we burn to tell, but especially for our wounds and hurts. Somewhere and somehow there ought to be an "Open End" where tears are understood and a heart beats for a common sorrow.

Typical of the hard-heartedness of an uncaring world is Sartre's description of hell: There each person vomits out his hate and woes and no one listens; everyone turns a deaf ear, waiting only to pour out his own pet peeves and show his own wounds. But no one listens; each one is concerned with his ego. As the curtain goes down, the last line of the play is, "My neighbor is hell." Hell is where there is no sympathy, no common concern, no care.

In the world of caring, two experiences give us a clue to the mystery of life. The first is a baby suffering, for example, from a burn. The other is a mother with a wayward daughter who takes to drink, thievery and LSD and calls her mother an "old hag" and brings disgrace to the family. In both these instances, neither the baby nor the daughter know how the mother of each is hurt. The infant is unaware and the daughter is indifferent.

But the same is not true of motherhood. Here there is what might be called "empathy" or the power of relating oneself to another to such an extent as to have one's emotions and feelings qualified by the other. A delicate awareness, like a magnetic needle, makes the mother's heart vibrate in unison with the woes of the offspring. Just as it is said that certain notes struck on a violin can break a glass, so, too, a heart can break without any tangible contact. What is more, the mother would, if she could, take the burns of her child onto her own flesh. But human flesh, while it is responsive to many touches, has a finite limit and impenetrability about it. The physical ailments of others we can "feel," but the flesh of one cannot take on the tatterings of flesh. Despite this, the desire of empathy is deep as the following story illustrates.

A Hindu passing by a farmer who was beating his ox, felt compassion for the animal to such a degree that at night he found the lash marks on his own back.

But the transference through empathy is greater in the moral order than the physical. Here empathy is realistic. In the case of the delinquent daughter, the mother may suffer more than the daughter, because the mother has a clearer idea of the gravity of the daughter's conduct. A physician by the side of a delirious patient with a high fever knows the condition of the patient far better than the victim of fever himself. In fact, the patient may insist that he is well and wish to get out of bed. The pig wallowing in the mud does not know that it is dirty, but the onlooker does because of a nobler idea of cleanliness. So, in the moral order, innocence understands sin better than sin itself. The one thing we never learn by experience is sin. The onlooker on moral disorder suffers more than the victim unless he is one of those callous souls who say, "No, I do not allow these things to affect me."

A human emotion remains to be considered in the case of the wayward daughter, and that is the hostility which the wayward daughter often feels for the mother. This exists also toward public order, authority and the upholders of righteousness by those who impugn decency. As Dorothy Sayers puts into the mouth of Judas, "There are too many in the world like me . . . I wanted to believe Him guilty because I could not endure His innocence. He was greater than I, and I hated Him. And now I hate myself. Do you know what hell-fire is? It is the light of God's unbearable innocence that sears and shrivels like flame. It shows you what you are. It is a fearful thing to see oneself for a moment as one really is."

Hostility can be intense for those who care; whether it be the daughter for the mother, the patient for the therapist, the delinquent for the counselor, or the fallen-away for the minister of God. But what is amazing is that despite all the poison exuded by the morally guilty, a process of absorption goes on by the one who cares; the returning of love for hate, the open arms for those who would nail. Always there is a hand lifted in forgiveness and a heart ready to embrace, and lips offered to a blistering kiss of betrayal. As James Hilton said, "If you forgive enough people, you belong to them and they to you, whether either person likes it or not . . . the squatter's rights of the heart." There is no space here to unravel the full mystery, but is there not an "open end" in the Universe itself where Love cares when the unloving do not, and where Love suffers when a child falls and a man tumbles?

Accepting Others

~§ A couple had waited for several years for a child, and then when it arrived an estrangement arose between the three. The husband thought the wife cared more for the child than for him; the wife felt the child was a kind of an intruder in the house and prevented them from traveling

as they had done for many years. The problem was acceptance, or how to relate to other people. The difficulty exists
in all areas of life, even in the relation of God to man; it
becomes acute in the face of a lifelong illness when one has
to decide whether or not to accept the will of God. In relation to man, it is acceptance; in relation to God, it is resignation.

Acceptance in all its forms is difficult, whether it be acceptance of our own limitations and failings, or the idio-
syncracies and oddities of others. It is easy to accept humanity; it is hard to accept "this" person. When two persons
are put in contact, there is the possibility that they may be
like the negative and positive poles of electricity, generat-
ing sparks of heat but no light.

Suppose one limits the problem to a readiness on the
part of one to be of help to another, such as a mother and
father when they try to relate to their teenage son and they
run up against a brick wall. There seems to be an impenetrability, a confusion of tongues, a readiness to help on the
one hand; a reluctance to be helped on the other.

Acceptance begins the moment there is a common de-
nominator between two persons. A psychological relation is
established when one of the parties feels a need to receive,
and the other perceives a need to give. Those who are well
have no need of a physician; those who deny that they are
wounded are not likely to welcome a bandage or a tourni-
quet. The final step is taken when one person comes to another for help. Naturally, unless there is a quest, the problem of acceptance does not exist.

A second condition refers not to the one seeking help,
but to the helper or the therapist. He must not start with
any prejudgments or fit the anxious person into a ready-
made category. The good Samaritan must have some vul-
nerability or sensitiveness in order to share the wounds and
fears of others; he must be like a blackboard on which

nothing is written. His attitude must be "I care enough for you to be able to share your feelings." As a scientist passively sits before nature and lets it unfold its laws, so the therapist must allow the patient to write the agenda. The counselor and helper must not be like a commercial saying to the distressed one before him, "Do you feel run-down, tired, exhausted, cranky, dissatisfied with yourself because people do not understand you? Take Livery's little liver tablets." There is no cure-all for the person seeking understanding. He is unique and, for the moment, no other person in the world exists but him.

A third condition which is possible even when one cannot "reach" another is to return love in place of the other's un-love; return his hating with caring, his rejection with acceptance. Generally we avoid those paths which we know are infested with robbers, but in true assistance, one must walk into plague, fires and drowning waters—risking all for the sake of another. At this point, there begins to be absorption of the evil of another which helps to diminish it. Turning the other cheek, instead of multiplying hate, kills it by not passing it back. One patient wrote of her therapist, "I began to understand that not only were you sensitive to the understanding of my feelings, but you also cared and cared much. . . . I tried hating and attacking you. But you were always there like a firm rock; I could plainly see that I could not stop your love."

The psychology of acceptance points up the theology of the redemption. One has to look for inspiration beyond the petty ego, to a Love that went on loving even during a crucifixion, and like a Divine sponge, sucked up the evil. The only place in all the world where Love truly loved those who apparently were not worth loving, and were even unlovable, is on the Cross. Here there is Love to the uttermost, swallowing up, gulping down, drinking deep the bitter chalice, taking the worst man had to offer, and then rising above it. This is the secret of all therapy for those who refuse to relate to us. As Russell Howe put it, "He is the Lord because He is God. But I know Him as my Lord because He let me kill Him, and then He came back."

The Adolescence of the Old

&s; The young think that the old are out of date; the old think that the young are immature. But one wonders if today there is neither young nor old, despite the age gap between the two. Is there not rather a new kind of adolescence which has nothing whatever to do with years, but centers on the problem of personal identity? "Who am I?" or "I am not myself" is a question or statement restricted neither to those whose shadows fall behind them, nor to those whose shadows fall in front of them. The inability to make adjustments to life, the absence of goals or targets, and the readiness to be swayed by every wind of opinion is the immaturity which knows no calendar.

The new adolescence may be described in the words of George Bernard Shaw, "I stand midway between youth and age, like a man who has missed his train: too late for the last one and too early for the next. What am I to do? What am I? I have no Bible, no creed; the war has shot both of them out of my hands."

The world has not grown old; it has become adolescent —it is at an in-between era, like the vacant page between the Old and New Testaments. Arthur Miller in *Death of a Salesman* makes Happy say, "Sometimes I sit in my apartment—all alone. And I think of the rent I'm paying. And it's crazy. But then it's what I always wanted. My own apartment, a car and plenty of women. And still . . . I'm lonely."

Adolescence is the lonely time of life, whether it be the moment when the ego begins to assert itself in the face of parental authority, or the time when the ego is disgusted with itself because it threw off all authority and became its own god. In the words of Clifford Odets, "A certain man once said that in our youth we collect materials to build a bridge to the moon, but in our old age we use the materials to build a shack."

This loneliness of the new adolescence is not external but internal; it comes not from want of companionship or friendship, but from a void inside. This estrangement is something new in our culture, and like pestilence, is indifferent to the age of cells.

Kenneth Keniston in his study of youth in American society, uses one word to describe them—"uncommitted." They dislike and distrust all institutional involvements which make them feel trapped; they survive only on the periphery of a group; they participate only by observation. They refuse, in a word, to commit themselves. But is this a quality only of the young? Has not Douglas Woodruff written on the uncommitted mind in relation only to adults? It used to be that the alienated youth could ask their elders for flags to march under, crosses to live under, and rules to live by; now the old adolescents have nothing to give them. They have no signposts either. Why ask the way of those who also are lost?

The New Adolescence then no more belongs to teenagers than to sexagenarians because it is a state of mind. Basically, it is a question of identity: "Who am I?" And the old no more than the young can answer the question.

How does one get out of this new adolescence? A negative and a positive way are both possible. The negative way to unveil our identity is to face up to shame. All feel it in varying degrees, either after an excess, or in contrast to the innocence of a child, or when rebuffed by the unshakably good, or even in the dark dreams of the night. Shame is self-exposure. It does not present us as we would like to be, but as we are. It strips us of pretensions and makes us hide as Adam and Eve hid after their sin. "We were naked and ashamed." They recognized their own identity or the image which they had spoiled, the portrait they had blotched. Shame is a self-confrontation, the open fork on the road, the forcing us to take another path; it is the mirror held up to our identity which does not flatter no matter how much we make the tongue flatter.

This self-disclosure in shame does not lie; sleeping tablets may be used to becloud the truth, but there is our identity as we stand now, and as we will stand before the Judgment Seat of God. And there is no adolescent in the world, young or old, who does not have this moment of disclosure of his identity.

The more positive way of solving the identity crisis is to cry out to someone to pick up the broken pieces and to put the Humpty Dumpty of our life together again. The split atom has brought on the split man. There must be some other way of healing the brokenness than "life with Benzedrine, sleep with Nembutal and happiness with alcohol." No one can pack a suitcase if he goes into the suitcase; as no one can make a United Nations except someone outside the nations.

So, in our split personality of the New Adolescence, there must be someone outside ourselves who can effect the reconciliation, whether it be the young who are old with disillusionment, or the old who are childish with meaninglessness. It may very well be that the most encouraging word that can be uttered at our present day is the word "sin." It is the battle cry of hope and liberation, the standard of victory and the gospel of cheer and encouragement. Once we recognize that the trouble is not with things *outside* us, but rather *in* us, God can do something to mend our broken hearts.

Adolescence

৺§ Adolescence is a coma. It is a period of suspension between years of childhood when one is dependent on parents and an adult age when one is dependent on a boss, a wife, or public opinion. It used to be an age that listened to the voice of experience; today adolescents regard their elders as the voice of inexperience.

Because adolescence is an interim period in life, or the pause that depresses, it is neither a psychotic state into which people are born, nor a neurotic state which they make for themselves.

There are two ways of being miserable: one is to do the things you are forced to do; the other is to do the things you choose to do. The second is pure or unmixed misery when one is pulled in opposite directions. This is sometimes found in unadulterated forms in pre-adults. Adolescents are unhappy because they are constantly being pulled by opposite forces such as:

1. The adolescent is on the one hand an imitator and on the other, a rebel. He seeks to be like others in his group, wearing the same kind of clothes, listening to the same type of music, using the same jargon; but he is also pulled in the opposite direction, seeking superiority either by having a car, or a better car than his fellows, or living in a better house, or one that is on the right side of the tracks.

2. The adolescent is torn between looking his worst and looking his best. The young girl will affect flowing hair, pants, low heels, as if in rebellion against the adult social order and its conventions, or else to attract attention. But, in another mood, she wants a new frock, the privilege of

putting her head in a steel trap to emerge with a different hairdo, and hopes the boy will give her a silver bracelet to go with her braces.

3. Another tension is that which develops between cockiness and timidity. The cocky feeling comes before one knows anything well, and the timid feeling from—well, that one knows nothing. The cockiness makes the adolescent refer to the father as "Oh him," but timidity makes him say "Ahem" to the father a dozen times before he asks for the car.

4. Silence and loquaciousness are other tensions. The adolescent feels lonely at home and can find nothing to talk about. But on the telephone, the adolescent can talk for hours.

5. The greatest tension of all is between two kinds of steadiness. The boy wants a car, not a borrowed one, but his own, one with which he can go steady. The girl wants a boy with whom she can go steady. The boy has a prepossession for possession; the girl has a prepossession to be possessed. But the boy soon wants a new model and peculiarly enough that affects the girl.

It might be well for teenagers to recall the words of Mozart and Victor Hugo. Mozart wrote to his father, "Nature speaks in me as loudly as in anyone else, and I believe with greater force than in the uncultured and gross. Nevertheless, I refuse to regulate my conduct on the same basis as some young men of my age. On the one side, I have a spirit sincerely religious; I have too much honor and too much love for my neighbor, to deceive any innocent creature. On the other hand, my health is infinitely too precious to hazard it in any passing fancy. I can swear before God that I can reproach myself with no failure."

Victor Hugo penned the same sentiments to his fiancée in 1820: "It is my desire to be worthy of you, that has made me so severe on myself. If I am constantly preserved from those excesses too common to my age, and which the world so readily excuses, it is not because I have not had a chance to sin; but rather it is that the thought of you constantly preserves me. Thus have I kept intact, thanks to you, the sole treasures I can offer you on the day of marriage; a pure body and a virginal heart."

Elders must not be too hard on the tensions of teenagers for they are for the most part biological. Elders have tensions too, which, in their criticism of teenagers they are apt to forget, namely, the tension between what they are and what they ought to be. It is for elders to teach youth that they have only one arrow in the quiver—that is the arrow of youth and it may be shot but once. Be sure that it hits the target—the Divinely appointed target—love of God, love of country, love of neighbor.

Teenagers

◆§ The term "teenagers" is not a particularly exact way to describe youth, because the span between thirteen and nineteen is too great. By seventeen generally the character of most youths is formed. A very well-known biographer of Napoleon stated that at fifteen "he was already formed; true, life had something to add to it, but all the defects and good qualities were there in his fifteenth year." Mussolini, fighting with his classmates when he was fifteen, had manifested the same characteristics that he manifested later on. He himself wrote, "I was then formed. I fear that the influences I underwent then were decisive."

If one puts garbage into the stomachs of children, it will be easy to forecast their health; if moral garbage is put into the minds of children, it is easy to predict how these ideas will become acts.

At a United Nations Congress on the prevention of

crime, it was strange that no one spoke out more strongly against all pornographic horror publications and immoral literature than L. N. Smirnov of the Soviet Union. He dealt with those who contend that to restrain immoral literature is to curtail freedom saying, "talking about human rights in connection with putting this degrading matter before juveniles, is like the devil quoting the Bible."

This does not mean that youth already bent in the direction of evil cannot become virtuous, for with the grace of God, nothing is impossible. But our present situation rather suggests that youth becomes acquainted with the knowledge of good and evil at too precocious an age. On the morning of an important battle, Napoleon took away from his tent a portrait of his son, the King of Rome. As the bitter struggle was about to begin, he ordered it removed, saying, "It is too soon for him to see a battlefield."

Youth presently is handicapped inasmuch as the major direction of their lives is in the hands of sociologists and psychologists, neither of whom have in their scientific equipment what Dr. Alexis Carrel says are the two essential conditions for developing character: isolation and discipline. Both of these come under the domain of religion and morality. As long as youths travel in herds with their eyes fixed on a one-octave banjo player, they are incapable of reconstructing themselves. As Dr. Carrel put it: "A mode of life which imposes on everyone a constant effort, a psychological and moral discipline and privation, is necessary. An ascetic and mystical minority would rapidly acquire an irresistible power over the self-indulgent and spineless majority." He goes on to say that without this moral self-denial, the intelligence itself becomes anemic. The problem then is not what to do with teenagers; it is who will train them in the Ten Commandments and morality before they are sixteen and seventeen.

Every adult forgets that he was once a teenager. One

wonders how many, if they thought about it, would like to return again to that turbulent, juvenile period. Teenage is like death; you cannot thoroughly understand it until you have passed through it. It is an age where one is torn between the desire to express one's own individuality, and yet to be identical with everyone in the group. That is why teenagers dress alike, talk alike, love the same music and the same dances. They are "in" the sheepfold at the moment that say they are shepherds. Never again in life will there be such a tension between freedom to express oneself and readiness to be a grape in the wine vat of teenage-icity.

From another point of view, teenage is a "change of life," a climactic period in which the biological drives which die later are now born with a tumultuous physiological and mental backwash. As the brain is affected by the withdrawal of vital forces later on in life, so in youth there comes another kind of hot flash—the alleys and gateways of the body open themselves to the unpredictable and the bizarre.

Teenagers are not the same in each period of history. They, therefore, must not be judged solely by standards foreign to their way of life. Neither must one see in them nothing but guitars, long hair, bony knees and studied unkemptness. As there are pearls in oysters, so there are treasures in their seeming darkness.

The teenager is right, to some extent, in acting the way he does. He would go mad in this world if he did not react against it by doing mad things; he would be frustrated and neurotic if he accepted the values of a modern civilization which his parents hold so dear—such as the value that life is for making money. Teenagers like money, but do not want to make it the main goal of life. Furthermore, though they have never analyzed it, they cannot see any righteousness in a system in which six percent of the population of the world controls forty-six percent of the world's wealth. They may not know how to equalize it, but they know that treating our affluent civilization as an island in the ocean of the world's poverty and misery does not make sense.

Teenagers never sat down and figured out the modern stupidities, just as they may never have analyzed the complexity of reasons behind the polluted air of cities, but they know it is there—they can smell it. They are right in their protests, but they have no reforms; their protests are immediate, emotional and without program. Revolutionists, they are, but not like the old Bolshevik revolutionists who knew what they would set fire to and what they would build on its ruins. They are protesters without programs, reformers without policy, engines without flywheels, full of resentment against an older generation which gave them ships but no ports.

The teenagers protest not only against the social and political injustices, but in a certain sense against the religious world as well. Religion generally does not touch them. In some instances this is due to their own want of morals which thrive in the dark and shrink from the light of betterment. But, in some cases, is it not because those in religion give more precepts than they do examples? If religion gives a code, youth wants to see that code lived out in the one who gives it. One cannot throw a book at teenagers. They see too often disproportion between the nobility of what religion teaches and the mediocrity of the lives of the teachers; so they excuse themselves from becoming involved.

Most teenagers who have gone to extremes in their confused and frustrated lives are little Augustines. Augustine wrote about his teenage excesses in his *Confessions.* He did everything the worst of teenagers ever did; he did more of it and more intensely. How did he survive and become so great? First, because he did a lot of reflecting. Most teenagers do not think; they just conform and imitate. Augustine advised teenagers to think for themselves, asking such questions as: "Why do you feel sad when you get violent either physically or erotically? Why do you squeal and stomp and shriek when you are with others like yourself, but not when you hear the same music alone? Why do you feel detribalized when you get outside the herd? Why do you dress like everybody else? Why do you want liberty without ever thinking whether it means doing what you *please* or what you *ought?* Can you get out of this sadness and moroseness by yourself? How high can you lift yourself by the lobes of your ear? Do you need outside help?" These reflections were the beginning of Augustine's greatness. Next he began to love—to love the neighbor, the poor person, the beggar, the sick boy, the unloved.

No one will ever convince teenagers by argument that they should know God and their souls. But let them go out and love the poor, the great unwashed, the sick, and they will find both God and their souls.

Teenage Personality

⋅§ What makes a teenager is the emergence of personality. Up until teenage, a youngster is part of a family, readily cooperating with its group actions and submitting to its authority. But, as soon as he becomes a teenager, there is a consciousness of his own ego, a deepening sense of personal responsibility and his differentiation from the family.

This sprouting of personality manifests itself in a trivial way, such as wearing identification, sporting loud socks, making loud noise to draw attention to himself. He will hardly speak in the family, though he will be on the phone for hours giving his ideas to fellow teenagers. Girls no longer play with boys; they curl up with novels and romances and movie magazines. The boy begins to carry a comb, scribbles initials of a girl on the desk, presses his tie, while the pimple on the end of the nose becomes a tremendous worry, particularly on the eve of a dance.

The adolescent is at his best in school and at his worst at home, because he is on his own in school. He seldom talks to "the old man" because "he does not understand." He is peevish with his mother because she does not treat him like a man. "She thinks I'm a kid." The family becomes like an armed camp. The boy hates his sister, but not the sisters of other boys.

But even a teenager is a contradiction. He wants to be himself, yet he refuses to be different from others. He asserts his own freedom yet surrenders it to a group. Completely given to imitation, his clothes, attitudes, moods and music are like those of his age group. Ridicule he cannot stand, and this drives him more and more into the destruction of his personality by merging it with an anonymous group. His extreme sensitivity reduces him to the size of an ant in a kind of a composite ant hill.

A survey of high school students revealed that thirty-eight percent considered that the greatest fault of any high school student was not to be one of the group, or to be considered an oddball. Therefore, some of the most favorite expressions of teenagers are: "Aw gee, Ma, none of the other kids are wearing one of those." "Oh, gee, Pa, everybody would make fun of me." "Oh gee, Ma, the other kids get seventy-eight dollars a week spending money."

The ego and personality which should develop is now lost in the impersonal mass of teenagers. This loss of personality at the very time personality should emerge, does not augur well for the future of democracy. This conformism, imitation, plagiarism, makes it imposssible for democracy in a future age to have leaders. Only eighteen percent of high school students admitted that they dared to be any different from the group. But when everybody thinks alike, there is no thought.

If there is any encouragement that parents should give to children when their personalities begin to emerge, it should be "Be yourself." Imitation is actually a desire for authority, but the authority is never defined. It always remains an anonymous authority. It is these same youths who will completely lose themselves in an anonymous authority who will complain against accepting the authority of Christ.

Why Teenagers Rebel

~§ The mood today is to give up on teenagers. Yet who does not know delinquents who became leaders in their community? The Gospels record an instance of this when Judas betrayed Our Blessed Lord and delivered Him over to the soldiers. There was much shouting that midnight in the Garden of Gethsemane, as He was being led away to the house of Caiphas. The excitement awakened a young man who impulsively ran out to see the excitement; the only thing that he had around him was a bed sheet. When he caught up with the officers who had just crossed over the Brook of Kedron, he saw that Our Lord was the prisoner. He began following Him, not just the crowd. Then he remonstrated with the officers who were arresting Him, probably telling them that it was unjust on their part.

The officer, already annoyed by what Peter had done by hacking off the ear of the servant of the high priest, and by the boy's too obvious sympathy for Our Lord, tried to arrest him. Being a teenager, he was much more agile than the police; he slipped out of his linen sheet and ran naked into the darkness.

Later on, this impulsive teenager is found in the company of Paul and Barnabas on their missionary journey. As long as they stayed on the blue waters of the sea and visited Cyprus, this teenager was an ardent missionary, but when Paul and Barnabas started going inland among robbers and mountain streams and dangers, this young man found the going too rough, and his missionary zeal ran out. He ran well at first, but he could not keep up the pace. Paul told him to go back to his mother in Jerusalem; but later on, the teenager comes through. Paul speaks of him as being a fellow worker and as being very profitable to him in the ministry. It must be remembered that this teenager who stumbled through life, found literary immortality, for he wrote the Second Gospel. His name was Mark.

Three youths once were expelled from their schools. One because he was always drawing pictures in geography class, the other because he was constantly fighting during recreation, and the third because he kept revolutionary literature under the mattress. No one today remembers the valedictorians or the bright boys of those classes, but there is no one in the world who does not know the first boy who was Hitler; the second, who was Mussolini; and the third, who was Stalin. How their teachers must have wished that they had been more patient!

Youth has higher aspirations than adults generally suspect, but adults do not challenge these aspirations, nor lead them to the heights. The young people today have a spirit of sacrifice and a readiness for surrender which has been untapped.

The Communists, the Nazis and the Fascists in the last generation knew how to appeal to the sacrificial spirit in youth. Youth is sick and tired of a milk and water liberalism which calls for no self-denial. But the elders fail to awaken that latent spirit.

Can an alcoholic father ever convince his teenage son to be temperate? Can a mother who has been divorced three times ever tell her teenage daughter that she must always be true to her word? Why not? Because reverence for a precept depends on reverence for the one who gives the precept. A teenager instinctively knows that if parents do not recognize any authority over him, then by what right do the parents command?

Teenagers do not ever state this clearly; they do not even know the instinctive reason why they rebel against their parents; but like little cogs, they rebel against the big cogs who refuse to do as they should.

The fourth commandment of God which is: Honor thy father and thy mother, is the link between the first three, which relate to our duties to God, and the last six, which relate to our duties as neighbors. From this commandment follows this truth: Parents who honor God always find it easy to train the children to honor them, the parents; children who honor parents always find it easy to honor the Heavenly Father. Juvenile delinquency will diminish when parents learn that God is not a swear word.

Hard to Be a Teenager

ᕔᔓ It is hard to be a teenager. I wonder how many adults would like to go through all the crises of adolescence again. George Bernard Shaw said that it was a pity that youth was wasted on the young. Jerome K. Jerome said to a woman who was thirty-nine, "I think it is a beautiful age—young enough not to have lost the joy of youth, old enough to have learned sympathy." Euripides, the pre-Christian Greek dramatist, praised youth as being the "best time to be rich and the best time to be poor." Shakespeare called teenage the "salad days when I was green in judgment." An English proverb takes another point of view: "Those who would be young when they are old, must be old when they are young."

To be a teenager is hard for many reasons. In our contemporary society, youth is interested in politics, social affairs, slum clearance and racial justice. Because the young see things either as black or white, their love of justice comes out negatively as a protest against a society which they believe tolerates these abuses. While this is all well and good in youth, a concern for the distressed entails no obvious deprivation, no spirit of poverty in cutting down their spending money. In fact, the young have the same tensions as religion often does when it fails to share its wealth with the poor.

Enduring no social hardships, they, too, pontificate against social abuses from ivory towers or from dens laden with a hundred discs. One finds this particularly in the "Great Unwashed" who protest against the society in which they live and yet in their workless days, depend on money sent to them by parents who could not afford to do so unless they lived in the society against which their "hippie" children rebel.

Adults see this inconsistency between blaming and helping much more clearly; that is why lucrative positions in life are often surrendered in order to serve the poor. Five doctors and professors in one medical school in the United States have practically given up their practice in order to serve in a clinic. Grown-ups clearly see that they must not protest unless they can reform, and they cannot reform unless their protest turns into some surrender of their possessions.

But does not even the protest of youth offer hope? Will not their present yearning for social betterment in the midst of their affluence later on turn to an abandonment of affluence in order to remake society? Certainly no previous generation of young Americans ever felt so keenly the need of becoming Good Samaritans to the peoples of rat-infested ghettos.

Did the present Jet Set ever have the same sense of responsibility to the poor in their youth, as the youths do today? They were probably devoid of a passion for social justice. The teenager of today will probably never lose his desire to make a better world; he will just sharpen it and work more cooperatively with all segments of society.

A second reason why it is hard to be a teenager is that his parents are now living in a world that is radically different from that of their youth when there were no atomic bombs, flights to the moon, or unravelings of the border line between chemistry and life. For them to say to their children, "In my day . . ." is nonsense. That day is gone forever. On the other hand, neither the parents nor the children have any idea of the kind of world we will be living in twenty years from now. Both the old and the young are facing the world of the future as they would a city in Europe which they had never before visited.

How is it possible to give directions or find one's way when there are no signposts? If children accuse parents of being "behind the times," parents might well retort that children are "behind the times" every year they live. Like the automatic rabbit in the dog race, technical progress always keeps ahead of them. For that reason, there has to be some guidance which is neither of the past nor of the future. The one thing is the teachings of the Gospel, which did not suit the times. The refrain rings out: "It has been said to you of old." Then comes, "But I say to you . . . Heaven and earth may pass away, but My Words will not pass away." Old and young can both drink of this fountain and become young again. Only something that does not suit the times can save the times.

Teenage Sensitiveness

⟨⟩ It is too bad that teenagers cannot write good autobiographies so that their keen sensitiveness would be revealed. But this is asking too much, since such writing requires standing off and viewing oneself from a distance and the perspective of time. Furthermore, as one ages one develops more humility and with it the ability to laugh at one's mistakes. We see others long before we see ourselves. In *The Scapegoat*, Daphne du Maurier wrote, "Someone jolted my elbow as I drank and said, 'Pardon me, please,' and as I moved to give him space, he turned and stared at me and I at him. I realized with a strange sense of shock and fear and nausea all combined that his face and voice were known to me too well. I was looking at myself."

Teenagers often go through a humiliation bordering on crucifixion through sensitiveness. What a tragedy is a pimple on the face, a skirt that is too long, a coat that is too short, the father who comes to the school with greasy overalls—overalls are all right, but not greasy ones—the mother who has an accent, the reprimand before the class, the indifferent look of a fellow student and, above all, the dread of being classified into the trinity of outcasts: as a "crumb, dumb or bum."

Standards are built into the life of teenagers, and conformism is rigid. An elephant apart from the herd is not as panic-stricken as one who dresses well when others do not, or who refuses to smoke pot when others do. The dread of not being like others makes them fearful of using their own judgment, of listening to an inner voice or of ever making a self-appraisal apart from the mob. There is a market price that is fixed, and every teenager must sell himself at that figure.

But, at the same time, the teenager has another drive which is the opposite of conformism. It is a desire to be an emerging personality, not a rubber stamp. His conformism is in part aided by a rebellion against being molded by elders, but his emerging individuality makes him sometimes wish he could be different. Teenagers are like ants who want to live in the swarm of the anthill, and at the same time, they would like to be the ant who is brave enough to go to a picnic alone.

This drive to be an individual is expressed in their poetry and songs which stress "I want to be me." The truth is, there is one sense in which the self most discovers itself and that is: *in serving and loving others.* When does a teenager become more conscious of his personality than after he has forgotten it by volunteering in a hospital, teaching dropouts, cleaning up slums and mowing the old widow's lawn? When his heart says, "I want to be for others," that is the moment when his sense of dignity and worth is at its peak.

The happy teenager is the one who balances this tendency to be absorbed in the lives of others, with the opposite drive to emerge as a unique person. This happens when teenagers are open to insights which persons other than their peers may give them about themselves.

Paul Nathanson, one father, tells of an experience he had in comparing his son's qualities with his own. Ten attributes or qualities were set down as the standard. Each agreed to mark those qualities in which he believed himself superior. In the final tally, the son believed himself superior to the father in seven attributes, below him in only one, and equal in the other two. The father was more generous to the son, but what resulted was a greater self-knowledge of each and a greater confidence in one another.

Generally, this mutual "give and take" is lacking. A

teenager rarely gets any correction after childhood. If a parent does give it, the answer invariably is, "But look what you do! You are not so faultless," as if the fault in another canceled out the fault in self. Elders, too, may be to blame by concentrating on the fault: "Look what you have done now," instead of inspiring confidence by saying, "What can we do now?"

The reconciliation of this contradiction in teenagers, to surrender oneself to the mob as a drop of water in a glass of wine, and to want "to be me" with no regard for others, is that Divine injunction: "Love your neighbor as yourself." "As yourself" implies a degree of self-love, self-respect, but instead of crawling inside a shell of egotism, one is to direct this personality outward, serving humanity and especially the poor. No one appreciates a final spiritual liberation so much as the one who has long been imprisoned in defeat and despair, and then discovers his true freedom. It is egotism that spoils us. Few indeed ever reach that humility which makes for greatness as the preacher who, when congratulated on his sermon by a gushing friend who said, "you were magnificent," answered, "The devil already told me."

Help for Teenagers

◆§ Anyone who has been privileged to read the diaries of teenagers will discover their tortures inadequately expressed, but poignantly felt. One writes, "I'm more and more bored with myself, and I don't talk as much as I used to. Girls don't understand me. I wish I could see Marie, the one I met last summer. She is the only one who would ever listen to what I say." From another teenager's diary, "Mom's too busy and she never listens. Dad says I will never amount to anything. I wish I knew what to do with myself. I look in the mirror and wonder, what is me? I could almost cry. . . . Mary said that no man would ever marry her with her bad teeth and pimples."

These are really tragic deliverances and these troubled souls are looking for ways out of these dilemmas. Perhaps a few suggestions would help:

1. Note the difference between what happens to you and the way you react to what happens. A little pimple appears on the nose and you go into a tailspin. Your emotions are running away with your reason. The emotional response must always be in proportion to that which prompted it, but never in excess of it. If a pimple gets you down now, think of what business routine will do to you in ten years. You will call it the "rat race." Every night, give yourself a few moments of quiet and force petty worries out of your mind. As a wise man wrote:

> On a branch that swings
> Sits a bird that sings
> Knowing it has wings.

2. Study those in school who are the most popular and those who are the most unpopular. Then ask yourself why? You will discover that the popular boy or girl is the one who is pleasant to everyone, who gives a helping hand to others and who never talks about himself. The unpopular youth is the one who high-hats almost everyone except his few friends, is sarcastic, and laughs at others' mistakes. If you want to be loved, stop loving yourself, or feeling sorry for yourself. When you get older you will find that even your sickness will last less long if you are surrounded by the thoughtfulness and love of others. Dr. Karl Menninger, the famous psychiatrist, once wrote, "You cure by atmosphere, by attitude, by sympathetic understanding on the part of everyone in the hospital." Most young people become unpopular by trying to be popular. Popu-

larity is a bridesmaid, not a bride; it is a by-product of considerateness of others. Narcissus loved himself and Echo loved Narcissus. But he kept staring at his own image in the pool and thus could find no time for her. Echo left weeping. Popularity is a feedback from self-forgetfulness.

3. Do not fall in love with an experience, but only with a person. This is difficult during teenage, because girls like boys and boys like girls. They enjoy the contrast of masculinity and femininity. Love is really love only when the object is a person. The trick is to distinguish between the person and the experience of feeling in love which the other engenders. Experiences are replaceable, but persons are not. No one can take the place of your father or your mother. You will often find that what makes you flip is a look, a kind word, a bit of attention or the touch of a hand. Never confuse the electric wire which gives you the shock with the manager of the Electric Light Company.

4. Grow up as quickly as you can, so that you do not fall in love either with masculinity or femininity. You have often heard about pinup girls. These pictures are sold by the hundreds of thousands, and they are all of the same girls. There is a world of difference between loving the general and loving the particular. One can love a garden, but few want a garden in the house as a life companion. Many love humanity, as did Rousseau, but he abandoned each of his children after birth. Love in the abstract is a world apart from love in the concrete. On the other hand, neither is falling in love with a fraction the same as loving a person. Many a man falls in love with a dimple and makes the mistake of marrying the whole woman. This does not mean that one should become so desperate that the boy takes everything he can get, and the girl takes anything she can get.

5. There are two kinds of love: need love and gift love. Need love is something every heart possesses. Just as the eye needs light, the ear sound and the stomach food, so every

heart needs love. But gift love is that which we bestow even when it is not needed. If you saw a little child on the street and in danger of traffic, your gift love would urge you to save the life of the child. Gift love does not help us directly; it helps others. Gift love makes us happier than being satisfied with need love. If you are ever generous enough to understand gift love, then you can understand why God came down into the muck and dirt of human life to teach us love—the love that goes on loving even when it is not returned.

Teenagers and Happiness

⋖§ A teenager develops like an icicle. When the icicle begins to form, its color is determined by the drops of water which enter into its formation. If the water is clean, the icicle is clear and transparent; if the water is dirty, the icicle does not glow. So with a teenager. Every thought, pure or foul in his or her mind, every act of kindness or hate becomes a part of character. Teenagers often wonder why their elders can foretell what kind of men or women they will make. The reason is that one need not throw a log into a stream to find which way the current is flowing: a straw will do just as well.

Every teenager wants to be happy, although when you listen to their songs, so full of a yearning for death, one sometimes wonders. But this sadness is because they are already spoiled and disillusioned. Yet before they allow the worm of evil to eat the apple of their lives, they really want to be happy. That is what the Beatitudes of Our Lord were about: eight rules for being happy, each one beginning with, "Happy are they . . ."

There are two ways to be happy though a teenager:

1. Do not monkey with the carburetor of your car. When you buy a car, a set of directions is given by the manufacturer, *e.g.*, when to grease it, oil it, etc. These instructions were never meant to cramp your style or destroy your freedom. Rather, like the advice of any professional, they are designed to enable you to get the maximum of pleasure out of the machine. The carburetor which controls the flow of gas into the cylinders is very delicate and finely adjusted; so you are told, "Do not monkey with the carburetor."

Your conscience is like the carburetor. God put into your conscience certain directions for leading a happy life, but if you heed others who tell you to follow them instead of your conscience, you will feel an inner unhappiness like the spitting of the motor if you fool with the carburetor. If you fail to heed these warnings, you may eventually get into a state where you will say, "Oh! There isn't any manufacturer of an automobile; these so-called directions are just man-made taboos. I want to be free from restraints." You will be! But you will be "free" like a pendulum freed from the clock—useless and unable to swing in the rhythmic joy of order and inner peace. Go on rebelling against the inner voice which is the voice of God, and you will feel frustrated, miserable, unhappy, and wish you were dead!

God has written a wonderful symphony for life, well-scored and easy to follow if we study the music. You will make a life full of harmony and will live in peace with the other musicians who are your fellow citizens, if you but heed the notes.

2. "Get out of your teenage nest as fast as you can." Teenage is really only a small bridge connecting childhood with maturity. It is a transition period, not a career. You happen to be living in a country which has the longest adolescence period of any in the world. One is not a teenager until nineteen; one is a teenager as long as he fails to mature into an acceptance of responsibilities.

All those who are destined for greatness get out of the period of immaturity as soon as possible. Meet the challenge in the world around about you. Be young men! Be young women! Because the word "teen" is still in nine*teen* it does not mean that you have to wait that long to realize that you are not here to have the world serve you, but for you to serve the world. In this adventure into responsibility, Heaven will help you. In the Book of Deuteronomy, we read that as the eagles stir in the nests of the young and hover over them, so God stirs and hovers over us. God's loving compulsion is aimed at effort. He "stirs up the warm nest of teenagers' irresponsibility" by the prickings of conscience, by the inner voice of the Spirit and sometimes by trial—anything to make us grow up. Otherwise, we would stiffen in juvenile habits, becoming mental dwarfs. The stirring of the nest is actually the sign of the closer approach of the Father guiding our lives. If we lay ourselves in God's ways—after having tried ourselves—He will see that no harm comes to us. Out of the nest, out of the cradle!

Teenage Respect

◆§ Some parents complain that their teenage children never obey them; other parents deny that they have any difficulties in this area. Why the difference?

The difference is not always in the children, as is too often assumed; it may lie in the parents. The rebellion against the authority of the elders is not always because teenagers are opposed to authority, but rather because of those who administer authority. St. Thomas Aquinas, one of the greatest philosophers who ever lived, gave this rule in Latin which is worth quoting: *"Ex reverentia praecipi-*

entis procedere debet reverentia praecepti." (The respect that one has for a rule flows from the respect that one has for the one who gives it.)

When it comes to music, for example, teenagers are very willing to accept the authority of a band leader, because they feel he knows his subject and is qualified to speak on it. The teenage boy will accept the authority of a well-known baseball player on the subject of sports, because his accomplishments are worthy of respect in that field. It was said of the soldiers of Napoleon that if anyone had cut out their hearts, they would have seen his image engraved thereon—so much did they respect his ability as a soldier.

Little boys never have any difficulty in accepting the authority of their parents. "My daddy told me" is their final word on any subject. Later on, when the little boy becomes a teenager, there is not that same spontaneous acceptance of parental authority; there must be added another reason for parental respect, and that is the moral worth of the one who gives it. Where there is love, because of the nobility of the character of the parents, there is obedience. Our Blessed Lord based obedience to His Commandments upon love: "If you love Me, you will keep My Commandments." Before He gave Peter the authority to rule over His lambs and sheep, He asked him three times, "Do you love Me?" Once there was a love admitted for Christ on the basis of His conquest over evil, then there would be no question whatever of obedience to His commands.

When a teacher lacks that moral and intellectual value which commands respect, disobedience results. The rise of juvenile delinquency is in direct proportion to the decline of moral values among the parents. If the parents of teenagers are intemperate, given to alcoholism, infidelity, quarreling and fighting, what can be expected of the children? If parents have made second marriages, with first spouses still living, it is impossible for these parents to say to their children, "You must keep your word and never break it";

the children know they have already broken a word concerning loving unto death. It will not do for alcoholic parents to say, "You must not drink," if the children have seen either of the parents drunk.

On the contrary, when parents set a worthy example for their children, obedience is not rendered by the children because of a fear of punishment, but rather because they would not hurt those whom they love. The commandment of God: "Thou shalt honor thy father and thy mother," implies honor in the parents. Honor is a recognition of the excellence of someone.

It would be quite wrong always to blame the children for failure to honor their parents. Honor and dishonor, love and aversion, respect and disgust are born in them, according to what they see in the parents. Sometimes it may be the duty of teenagers to educate their parents. To parents who have not given good example, the teenagers must be given this counsel: The last generation has failed you; but you must not fail the next generation.

Teenage Love

◦§ A sixteen-year-old boy who was "madly in love," begged his parents to invite the parents of his girl friend to the house. When told that it might not be wise to plunge too quickly into marriage, he answered his parents, "Yes, but you do not know what love really is." This kind of argument is given generally by two classes of people—teenagers in love and enthusiasts of cubistic art: "You don't understand it." Instead of proving what they know, they argue that you are unknowing. The trick is not so much to show that they are omniscient, but rather that others are nescient. Perhaps teenagers might be spared dangerous plunges into unhappiness, did they but know a "few facts of life." Here are some questions they might ask themselves to sharpen their understanding.

1. "Am I in love with a person, or am I in love with love?" There are certain experiences which are absolutely new to youth. Because they are associated with the glands, the blood cells and generally with what are called passions, they force themselves upon youth with a violence and intensity which are apt to destroy reason and judgment. When a man is being chased by a wild bull in the field, it is hardly the moment to decide whether he will make his money by being a banker or labor leader. Similarly, a youth who is enjoying an initial experience might inquire if he loves what another person excites in him, or whether he loves the person.

2. "Do I realize that sex is replaceable, but love is not?" The mere enjoyment of passion as such can be indifferent to persons in its grip, but love can never be indifferent. No one can ever take the place of a mother, a father or a best friend. When they are gone, the niches remain empty for the rest of life. But the mere enjoyment of food can be experienced with a great variety of dishes. It is easy for youth to feel that the first one who ever aroused a feeling of love is the only love that is possible. One might just as well drink milk out of a bottle all his life, because the satisfaction of taste first came through a bottle. Some indeed do retain this devotion to a bottle; it corresponds with "going steady" with the first person who ever excited a gland. But if a person is loved, rather than the emotion, then that person is loved without change or alteration *"until death do us part!"*

3. "Do I think that the passion and the romantic feeling I have for a 'steady' now will endure with ever-increasing depth and intensity?" If this be true, why don't the parents of teenagers act toward one another like teenagers act toward one another? It is doubtful that the teenager has a

power which no adult ever possessed. But the teenager assumes that passion is something that will enrich the organism through life, will fill it with endless transports, ever more intense and gratifying. Hunger for food is to some extent like the hunger for love. Why are there more ulcers at forty than at fourteen? Why do men, when they get old, give up fried foods? Something happened to the hunger; something like that happens to all hungers, with the possible exception of avarice. This does not mean that love decreases as time goes on; but it does mean that the biological and erotic accompaniment of love decreases. Therefore, one has to make sure that it is a person and not a "thrill" that one loves.

4. "If I fall in love with an 'ideal,' will I marry a 'fact'?" The ideal has the nature of the infinite about it; because it is a dream, it surrounds itself with the dimension of eternity and unending bliss. Nothing sets a limit to a dream. But in marriage, the ideal begins to be a fact; what was the ideal, becomes "cabined and cribbed and confined." The great luminous desire is now reduced to a concrete image. The fog has lifted.

In other words, every woman promises a man that which God alone can give; every man promises a woman that which God alone can give. They are right in having the ideal; they are wrong in thinking that the other partner can give what heaven reserves for itself alone. The best of human love is only a spark which fell from the great Flame of Love, which is God. Marriage is not an experience in which there is an exchange of mutual egotisms, and in which the bond lasts only as long as the other gives a thrill; rather it is a symbol of a great mystery—the mystery of God Who fell in love with man and took upon Himself a human nature—forever. Marriage representing that eternal union, therefore lasts *"until death do us part."*

Sex and Love

&. Sex is rapid, but love requires patience and effort. Love is something like prayer—the daily invocation to the highest, and the rising above self, the struggling against selfishness, the hard quest for daily bread. Like prayer, it is not always answered, but the price of sex is so low that it is not beyond the price of any man's pocket, and its fruits can be tasted without delay.

Every human being has a sense of incompleteness; that is why he seeks out a fellow creature in order to fill up his own lack. But physical union of itself does not necessarily bring completeness, for even after the most intense physical union, there can be a deep sense of separateness and aloneness. For a few brief moments it may seem that one has penetrated into the very core of the one that is beloved; that nothing belonging to the other is hidden from self, but soon one discovers that this is not true. The ego is often confronted with its loneliness at the point of its maximum satisfaction.

Nothing indicates the difference between sex and love more than the fact that a man can be sexually attracted to a woman without being in love with her. And equally he can be in love with a woman without having the same sexual attraction to her that he might have to another.

Love is focused in what might be called the heart; sex is focused only in bodily pleasure. The more one becomes preoccupied with sexual desires, the more he concentrates upon his ego. The interest in the other person is only in the pleasure that other person gives, but not the person itself.

Love, on the contrary, takes us out of ourselves and

awakens a profound interest in the other human being. Hence, love always leads to service.

Another difference between sex and love is that the former is interested in the general, or the representative of the group, rather than in a helpmate to the soul. Soldiers with pinups in their barracks have no special affection for the individual pictured; the photograph is only a "sample" of a class or a herd. Girls who fall in love with a uniform, or a special kind of hairdo in boys are really concerned more with masculinity or popularity than with Beattle Benny. In both cases, it is function, not person; union not community which attracts.

As a writer on marriage has put it: "Lust is the enemy of love. It is like a wild boar wallowing among lilies. It is an attempt to snare the music by breaking the lute. It is the beast who sleeps after it has gorged its prey. Just as war is not for the sake of the loot of the private soldier, so the goal of life is not just the pleasure of the organisms. Young men are not called to be useless drones who gorge the hive's best honey.

Passion mistaken for love desires to take life and ends in mutual slaughter, whereas love, craving to give life, discovers itself in another generation."

The Mystery of Sex

✥§ Nothing smells worse than a lily that festers. Nothing so much harms youth as the loss of mystery in life. Sex is mystery, and that is why it is akin to religion in its depths. But how is it a mystery? A mystery is freighted with two inseparable aspects: one physical, the other spiritual; one visible, the other invisible; one known, the other unknown. Other things in life have this mysterious quality; a word is a mystery: physically it is a series of vibrations which a dog can hear better than a man; spiritually, the word has "meaning" which the dog does not understand, but man does.

A handshake is a mystery. If I clasp one of my hands with the other, there is no mystery, but if I clasp yours, there is. The latter has an invisible content which the first does not, namely, greeting or friendship. A kiss is a sacrament, or a sign of affection, but its invisible meaning is gone, is violently stolen by a stranger. Religion has many sacraments, such as baptism, in which a material thing is used as a vehicle for the communication of the spiritual.

Sex is a mystery because there is something physical about it and known: everyone is male or female. But there is something spiritual about it too, for sex is the deepest channel by which the love of one person communicates to another. That is why sex is no mystery to animals; it is physiological, seasonal and biological. A rooster never gets a neurosis because a hen does not love him; a pig is never psychotic because a sow makes eyes at another pig.

Only in man does that mystical quality enter, in which sex becomes the last surrender of a person to a person. To separate the physical from the personal is profanation of the sacred, a kind of sacrilege, like throwing a firebrand into a church just to enjoy the heat, the crackle of flame, the tumbling edifice and the seeming conquest at the sight of carbon and ashes.

The mystery of sex is also revealed by contrasting it with eating. Why is it no one ever minds seeing people eat in public, such as at a sidewalk café in Paris or at a picnic, but there is an inner revulsion at seeing lovemaking or sex practiced in public or in the theater? Why? Because eating does not have that inner quality of being deeply personal, but making love does. Sex being the most vibrant chord of love, it involves just two persons. To take that which is personal and make it public, or to expose it to the crowd or what in Latin is called the *vulgus* is to make it common; this is the essence of the vulgar—the profanation of a secret.

In reacting to the Victorian era in which sex was taboo, we arrived at the other extreme when it was contended that if we only brought it out in the open, we would do away with all the neuroses and sickly notions attached to it. Well, it has been publicized, propagandized and magnified, but we are not more normal. We analyzed the meter, but lost the meaning of the poem. We proved that a violin sonata is only the drawing of the hair of a dead horse across the entrails of a dead cat, but somehow we lost the ravishments of harmony.

C. S. Lewis has beautifully portrayed how this loss of mystery has ruined sex. "You can get a large audience together for a striptease act—that is, to watch a girl undress on the stage. Now suppose you came to a country where you could fill a theater by simply bringing a covered plate on the stage, and then slowly lifting the cover so as to let everyone see, just before the lights went out, that it contained a mutton chop on a bit of bacon. Would you not think that in that country something had gone wrong with the appetite for food? And would not everyone think there was something equally queer about the state of the sex instinct among us?"

Why is it that parents find it so difficult to explain sex to their children? Not the physiological side, that is easy enough, but the deep meaning of the love which exists between them. Being invisible and spiritual, this is difficult to communicate. There is a world of difference between prose and poetry, between the organic and the personal. Sex will either be a mystery, or else it will be the kind of theater on Broadway to which you cannot take your children.

The Case for Chastity

ଓ୶ There is a whispering campaign going on against chastity. The young are told that it is bad to repress themselves, that self-expression is always good. This is really a trick in words because there is never any expression without a repression of some kind. To repress the desire to rob a bank is to express the virtue of honesty; to repress a desire to drink too much alcohol is to express sobriety and good sense.

Other times it is said, "Everybody's doing it," and that "It doesn't make any difference anymore." Morality is not made by numbers. Communism is not right because it succeeds in repressing everyone in China.

One of the great dangers of pre-marital experience is that it causes conflicts in the boy and the girl. They cannot separate the early experience which gave satisfaction with the later experience of mature, personal and intellectual satisfaction.

And as regards frustration, here is the statement of one woman who had gone through the extra-marital experience and wrote, "Much is talked of the evil of frustration in the case of the woman who denies herself the physical expression of love. In my opinion that vague and generally periodic torment is nothing compared to the frustrations suffered by a woman who seeks happiness in love outside of marriage . . . it is a trapped, blind alley feeling that only one who has experienced it can appreciate. The conflict set up as a result of it is keen and distracting and almost from the outset casts its dark shadow over an experience which one had expected to be all light and freedom."

Very often such people are worn out before they are

thirty, and have never touched the deeper aspects of happiness. Overstimulated, and wrongly stimulated, they cannot later respond to normal marriage relations and the chances of compatibility are poor. Any divorce of the sexual experience from the spiritual experience is bound to create a disturbed mind. As one doctor put it, "Promiscuity makes people lose the greatest experience in life, love."

Pre-marital experience also destroys certain inhibitions in the young, which prepares them for infidelity later on in life.

Men and women living in chastity are very well balanced psychologically and physiologically. But there are innumerable cases of men and women living anything but chastely who are tortured by sexual obsessions and psychic conflicts. Continence is in no way damaging to the human being.

A very strong case could be made out also for the fact that those who contain themselves allow their energy to spend itself in another direction. It often does produce creativity, either artistic, or literary, and especially compassion for the poor.

Purity is not something negative, just as pure water is not the absence of dirt. The pure diamond is not merely the absence of carbon. Purity is a reverence for a mystery, and the mystery is that of creativeness. God has given to man and woman a terrific power of prolonging creation, of begetting new life. One, therefore, will always be reverent about the use of this power until God determines when it shall be put to work.

God is the Master of all circumstances of life. Each life is affected in what may seem the most ordinary way, by what is actually His Divine Plan.

An essayist made this startling statement: "What a sad age this is in which one makes his First Holy Communion to be through with religion, receives his college degree to be through with study, and marries to be through with love."

Sex Revolution

⋙ "Sex Revolution"—such is the description of the new society in which youth boasts that it will no longer be troubled by "taboos, myths and morals," and the thousand and one fences which keep them from poaching on others' property. We may have, by the same logic, other kinds of revolution, *e.g.* "Traffic Revolution" when everyone runs through red lights, or a "Murder Revolution" in which the mugging and murders of today will become so general that we can invoke the same law: "everybody's doing it." With the corruption and dishonesty in business and in politics, our "Dishonesty Revolution" cannot be far around the corner.

True, the Victorians said too little about sex, but are not we saying too much? It was said that if we did away with prudery, we would banish all problems about sexuality. But it has increased our problems, and to such an extent that sex has become intellectualized. Now we wallow in it as it becomes a flat surface. As Robert Fitch wrote, it is "like a cock crowing on a dunghill, not to salute the dawn but to glorify in an apotheosis of carnality, the filth on which he stands."

It is affirmed that we are in an age which is no worse than other days of erotic excesses. This is a half truth. People indeed were bad, even in the days of great faith. In the Middle Ages, the stones burst forth into Gothic Cathedrals. But there was this difference: in those days, they knew they were immoral. They admitted both the law and the fact that they broke it. Today, we not only break the law, but we deny the law. In those days when men had a cancer, they called it a cancer; today we call it health. Every criminal knew he was a criminal. Louis XIV, Richelieu and others did not claim that their actions were moral. That was one of the reasons why civilization stood while some individuals fell. The few in former times who broke the moral laws were considered off the reservation; today those who break the moral law are considered on the reservation, and those who keep it are considered off.

It is wrong to call it a Revolution in Morals; it is rather a Revolution in Culture. The upheaval in morals is merely the top of the iceberg; the four-fifths hidden beneath the surface of life represents culture. Life today is full of frustrations. The soul has no home. The flesh gives an immediacy of release to this emptiness, and makes us forget the loss of the meaning of life, while promiscuity acts as a kind of opium to the emptiness resulting from excesses.

It is not a Sex Revolution as such. There have been many of those in history in the past, such as at the close of the Middle Ages. The reasons why it is not a Sex or Moral Revolution are the following:

First, sex today is intellectualized, thought about, advertised. It has moved out of the glands into the brain; it has lost its natural expression and turned into a kind of mania or obsession. Its devotees are like those who say of television, "I hate it," but they go on looking at it.

The perverse forms which the so-called Sex Revolution has taken proves that it is not natural, but rather abnormal. The glorification of homosexuality, the turning of love into dread drudgery of constant searching and trysting, the murders which are associated with it in plays and novels are almost like talking about food in terms of garbage, and health in terms of leprosy.

Girls in college relate it often to status—hence the contempt and the ridicule of other girls because they have not trafficked away their virtue. Boys, too, pride themselves on the number they have ruined. Sex has thus become snobbery. It is almost like stealing fruit from another's garden

—not to eat, but to boast at a robbers' convention of how many rotten apples are in your barrel.

The justification that is given for immorality is often psychological, namely, to escape repression which is harmful. In other words, sex is wanted for non-sexual reasons. It would be very much like a man entering religion for the sake of the money he could make out of it. As love of God and neighbor, in this instance, would not be the primary reason, so sex is not the primary reason for this so-called Moral Revolution. It is the cultural emptiness, banality, frustration and meaninglessness of life in which we live. Not knowing why one is here or where one is going, some seek to escape from the so-called culture of our time with its atomic bomb, its mass civilization, its hangovers, psychoses and neuroses, through something primal, basic, elemental and primitive. It is a curious twist of human nature that it should fill up the emptiness of the soul with the husks of flesh. Sex is not wanted primarily; something else is wanted, and sex is the substitute for that other thing. It is not the other person who is wanted, but some fleeting seconds of escape, thanks to the other person.

This relation between frustration and sex madness was manifested in economic depressions and political revolutions. It is a way out—a search for security. As psychologist Georgene H. Seward put it, "People in our competitive individualized society have an exorbitant need of affection and reassurance. It is this need for human response, rather than genuine sexual desire which leads them into the tense, clutching types of relationships so prevalent among us. Sexual possession of another somehow assures an individual and bulwarks his ego defenses, taking the place of a partnership based on mutual love."

Why is sex so difficult to talk about, and why doesn't sex education completely solve the problem? The argument for giving youngsters sex education is that it will keep them from harm. It is pleaded: If you knew the effects of typhoid fever and you saw a quarantine sign on a house, would you not stay away from that house? Well, youngsters will avoid dangers and pitfalls of sex once they are told about them.

The analogy is not sound. First of all, no one has a typhoid attraction, but everyone has sex attraction. No one is inclined to break down the door and invade the privacy of such a diseased person; but the same cannot be said of the erotic appetite.

Furthermore, sex is not digestion or any other body function. It rightly is called a mystery. And what is a mystery? A mystery is something which has two sides: one that is known and another that is unknown. One is visible and the other invisible, one physiological, the other spiritual. The physical, visible side of the mystery is that every person is either male or female. The spiritual, invisible side is that this difference in sexes also implies love.

If the biological fact of eating and the biological fact of mating are the same, why is it that we do not mind seeing people eat in public, but we shrink from seeing lovemaking in public? It is because lovemaking is something reserved by one person for another, and involves secret communication. To expose the personal to the public, the secret to the *vulgus* or crowd is to render it vulgar.

A boy becomes a man the day he resents his mother, in the presence of other people, putting a handkerchief to his nose and saying, "Blow." He has come to a personal stage where he knows that there are certain things every man must do for himself. To take that which is reserved for the sanctuary of human life and to placard it at the crossroads of the world, is to profane the sacred.

Herein lies the essence of the obscene: the divorce of sex and love, the physiological from the spiritual, the biological from the mysterious, the common from the personal. Because of this double element, parents have difficulty in communicating a true knowledge of sex to their children; this difficulty is inherent in all sex education. What is communicated is only the scientific, the physical, the corporal. But what cannot be communicated to children is how this common fact is hidden in love, and how it is used to express love in those deeper moments when words fail. Sex is then a breath in the atmosphere of an abiding love and a life-long bond in which soul communicates with soul as well as body with body. Plato, speaking of knowledge, compared it to a man in a cave. What he saw were the shadows of figures passing in the daylight, leaving their shadows on the wall. In sex, the shadow or the biological is often seen, but the spiritual escapes. When only the physiological is consid-ered, it is natural for the young to think that sex is an ani-mal function, for does not exactly the same act prevail in the animal kingdom? Since pigs and roosters and goats have sex, and we have sex, are we not to do what comes natu-rally? Why introduce morals? What difference is there be-tween a pigsty and a bedroom of a husband and wife?

The first difference is that the animal mates when in sea-son; man, however, has not just biological urges. He has reason and will. Endowed with human freedom he lives not in a barnyard, but in a universe where there is a respect for the dignity of other persons and where love is bound up with liberty. It is the tremendous power of the word "no" which gives so much thrill to the word "yes." The more instinct rules, the greater the promiscuity and the less rela-tion there is with a person. One of the reasons boys look down on "pickups" is because there is wanting that delib-erate choice which is the mark of the person. Girls resent having attentions forced upon them, because they have been deprived of the power of choice which is essential to love. Even prostitutes develop a completely detached at-titude from those whom they serve because they know that they are only in an animal relationship without any love. They sometimes come to justify their lives saying that they just fulfill a biological function, and hence they are not doing wrong to any person because there is no love involved.

Animals fulfill only biological functions and when persons do the same, they are like batteries that can be substituted one for the other, or facial tissues which can be thrown away when used. One even finds this absence of the respect for persons in professions. Some doctors have no personal interest in patients—they love only the disease; some social workers and even clergymen are interested not in the afflicted person, but in "the case."

A further proof that human relationships are not only biological is the storm that a brother will put up if any boy abused his sister. "Hey, stay away, she's my sister." But is not the animal with whom he has had biological relations someone else's sister? What a storm of protest would go up from a family of children if the mother were attacked on the street! If we are animals, why protest? If we protest then it must be that somewhere inside each of us is an image of God; we are persons, each with the right of self-determination, so much our own that no one else in all the world is exactly like us.

Another reason why human sexual relations are not animal, and that we are not justified in doing what comes naturally, is our sense of shame. How many a young man after having plucked an unripe rose and trampled it under foot will say, "I forgot myself." Forgot what? To be an animal? Or did he forget to be a person? What was automatic and physiological as in seduction and rape is not human at all. Animals do not have this remorse, nor does it exist in marriage because in marriage the atmosphere of love is kept up for a lifelong relationship. Outside of it, one wants to be lost in the other person, but one finds himself thrown back on self, more lonely than before. No dog ever had a psychosis from being a sex maniac, nor a rooster a psychosis from running after chickens. Why not? Because there is no spirit in them as there is in man; because being made for the physical alone, the physical is natural. It takes eternity and the destiny for eternity to make a man despair. Because he has wings, man becomes frustrated when he wallows.

Sex and Death

ॐ The young in our civilization think of dying; the old refuse to think about it. The young sing about it, and their movies satirize death and war. They are very concerned with such issues as death on the highway and nuclear suicide. But the old pretend that death does not exist; they make the time of mourning as brief as possible, and feel awkward in the presence of death.

The cause for both the juvenile preoccupation about death and the adult evasion of the subject are one and the same, namely, life is accountancy. April fifteenth always lies ahead when taxes on the income of life have to be paid. This can be a very uncomfortable thought if one has been cheating. Deny it as much as we please, we know there comes a day when the balance sheet must be struck. The Book of Life will be closed and no further credit entries may be made. But it is the thought of debits which frighten —those daily letters conscience dropped on our doorstep and which we threw into the cellar of the unconscious, and our dreams threw them back in our faces.

Though there is a natural fear of extinction, that fear is heightened when the game of life has been played outside the foul lines. The young who are not yet clever enough to muster arguments against the final reckoning, mock it; the old know all the arguments against it, and are never completely convinced. Life plays peculiar tricks on us; what we suppressed in the subconscious, comes out where it should not, just as toothpaste, if the tube is pressed with the cap on, will come out we know not where.

Hence the elders who write literature make life so tragic, so sad, so absurd. Hemingway, who tried to swagger his way through a meaningless life with blood and revolution, could not cure his own spiritual bankruptcy except by blowing his head off. The poems of W. H. Auden often take place in a saloon "where business looks up to the barman when necessity is associated with horror, and freedom with boredom." Literature, too, has succumbed to the modern mood of showing the scars of the operation of life. Thomas Mann did it by finding salvation in despair, and James T. Farrell and Franz Kafka sought redemption in loneliness and anonymity. Without sharing such views, T. S. Eliot described this kind of mortal anxiety as a "Wasteland" full of dead souls, and dead cities with dead gods to watch over them. This is but a literary expression of the basic idea in the Apocalypse of St. John, "You call yourselves living, and yet you are dead."

Here is the key: There are two meanings of life and two meanings of death. In the Greek version of the words of Our Lord, "Whoever would save his life must lose it, and whoever loses his life for My sake will find it. For what doth it profit a man if he gain the whole world and lose his soul." The two Greek words used for life are "psyche" and "Zoe." Psyche is what gives us biological and psychological life. Zoe is the universal unending life of God which He gives to creatures who refuse to give up an orchard for a peach. The same is true of death. One word for death is biological extinction; the other is the death of sin which causes unceasing rot; sometimes it is called "the second death." Thus, there are two kinds of corpses: those ready to be put into the ground, and those whose souls are dead, but whom we bump up against at a cocktail party or on the street, apparently so very much alive.

The secret of a happy life is to see that as life goes on we become less concerned with having, and more with being; less fanatical about making a success in life and more about making life a success; less intent on the stops in the journey of life and more on the destination.

Could it be that locked up in this womb of time, we shrink from having an angel roll away the stone that opens to the Light of the Day that has no night? But after a good life, may not the vision of this other world be such as to make us brave the parturition by saying, "Oh death, where is thy victory; oh death where is thy sting." Nothing makes life so wonderful as a belief in the resurrection where one finally becomes reconciled with life, with God and with oneself, and where we know even as we were knowing.

Teenagers Talk to Parents

ে "Sit down now, Mom. Sit down now, Pop. I am going to give you a talk about the facts of life, and about the birds and bees.

"We teenagers are looked upon as a race apart, like one of the satellites floating about the sky. We are not supposed to be part of this world at all. The point I want to make is that we are part of the world, and particularly part of your world. And now, in the name of teenagers, and as a representative of many youngsters in the United States, I am going to tell you why we are the way we are.

"Instead of making adolescence a transition period— necessary, valuable, comical—preparing us for adult responsibilities, you made it a separate way of life.

"Our intellectual training is too slow; our social speed-up is too fast. Instead of allowing us to be individuals, we are catapulted into half-baked adults. Girls go from pigtails to cocktails, from heaven's natural bloom to cosmetics, and from bare feet to high heels. Boys go from collecting stamps to playing post office.

"Advertising is addressed to us on the assumption that we determine sales; music is geared to our immaturity. That is why you adults complain that you cannot find good music on the air. Forums are held for us, and we are asked to command before we have learned to obey.

"All culture declines when youth acquires a value in itself, and is not seen in relationship to the community. The wheat in the field, the apple on the tree, the corn on the stalk, are not plucked when they are unripe. They flower and they prosper only in the great community of the earth, the sun, the field, the moisture and the rain. Only then do they begin to acquire an independent value in the granary and the bins.

"So it is with us. We are plucked too green, unripe, unfinished, and as a result, some of us never grow out of being teenagers.

"A survey revealed that when the twist was popular with us, more adults succumbed to the craze with more horrible sacroiliac consequences than any of us teenagers. In olden times, the aged were spoken of as having a second childhood. Now the adults often have a perpetual teenage.

"You have given us a physical heritage, for we share your health; you have given us a social heritage, for we move among your friends. But we teenagers are beginning to ask ourselves if you have bequeathed to us a spiritual and moral heritage.

"Take your eyes off us for a moment. Too long have you regarded us as intellectual problems. You spend millions investigating teenagers as if you were research happy. Please do not make us statistics! There are too many experts. We want you, Mom and Pop, to put our education in the hands of amateurs—you."

A Teenager Talks to His Parents
of Responsibility

&ea§ "You say we have no responsibility. You are the products of progressive education; we are the by-products. You were brought up in a progressive school under the influence of John Dewey. He was America's great emancipator in the sense that he emancipated your generation from any subservience to either Church or State. You were taught that there is no obligation to anything except society, and that you were not to submit to authority. You were told you have no responsibility except to democracy.

"The difference between your generation and mine is this: You were taught there was no responsibility except to society, but you did not practice it. We practice it, and we are called delinquents. You lived in a world of theory; we live in a world of practice, and all we are doing actually is eating the fruit of the tree which you planted.

"Because you were raised in a spirit which denied responsibilities, you began shifting the burden of responsibility to the school and told the teachers that they were responsible for us. But they, too, were trained for the most part the same way as you. You were taught that everything is justifiable and that there is to be no discipline. It was said that everyone must practice self-expression. The child who smeared paint on a canvas was called an artist. Ungrammatical idioms were permitted because they were so expressive and one was not to correct a child lest he should feel inferior.

"What was omitted from your education was experience, reasoned demonstrations, the value of prohibitions such as 'stay away from that fire,' or 'don't run across the street in crowded traffic.'

"You just thought it was an interesting theory to be told, 'Always do what you want to do.'

"What are the results of this denial of responsibility? There is no one to whom we owe anything. We do not owe anything to God, because we may not mention His Name in school. We do not owe it to society, because society is as mixed up as we are. We thought we owed it to you, but you shifted the blame to the school. So, what do we do? We have to have some standard, and we have taken a smaller society than the nation—namely, our gang, our group of friends, our fellow teenagers.

"There is, therefore, no standard outside of ourselves, no one to whom we are responsible except to ourselves. It just happens to be a smaller society than Dewey's.

"A survey made at Purdue University revealed that fifty-one percent of us teenagers did everything to please either our friends, or our gang. So instead of conforming to the Commandments, as did our forefathers, we have our own commandment. That is why we dress alike, we talk alike. That is why we pretend to like the same kind of music, and have the same heroes. We have to have some sense of responsibility. Where else can we go except to ourselves?"

The Short Trip and the Long Pull

⊷§ Taking a trip today does not mean covering distance, but rather a descent in depth through a loss of conscience and consciousness. The self is too much with us quick and soon, to paraphrase the poet. The problem is how to get away from it: "Stop the world, I want to get off." "It's a

mad, mad, mad, mad world." How are we to find peace,
release from tensions, surcease from an uneasy conscience
and the sense of guilt and futility?

Two answers are possible to this problem of finding
inner peace and happiness. One is through the Short Trip,
the other the Long Pull. One is through the artificial destruction of reason and consciousness; the other is through
a slow life process of self-denial and inner repose through
union with the Ultimate.

The Short Trip strangely enough is usually taken by
those who are disgusted with life before they have even
begun to live it. They are like passengers on a ship who,
after experiencing the slow first mile in the harbor, decide
that the sea voyage is not worth taking and jump over-
board. The passion to telescope eternity into a moment is
in sharp contrast to those who overcome the weariness of
life by a permanence of struggle to the goal. The most
notable characteristic of a baby is that he tolerates no inter-
val between a desire and its satisfaction, between the urge
to be fed and the bottle in his mouth. What the baby
wants, he wants now. No intervals! No "Will be back in an
hour." This absence of a moratorium is what keeps parents
walking floors at midnight.

The drug addicts, the alienated youth who go in for LSD
or other such drugs suffer from this infantilism. They have
refused to become adults. They cannot wait for sex; they
carry plucked flowers because they cannot wait to plant or
cultivate them. Everything is plucked in that wild dash for
immediacy. They cannot wait to finish college, so they become dropouts. Perpetual infants, they would break the lute
to snare the music. Even passion becomes impulse, or "out-
let seeking." The catharsis through self-abnegation which is
essential for real expanded consciousness, is thwarted by a
carping criticism of others. Pleading love for everyone, in
their going around in "circles," they develop a hatred for
"squares." It is all done synthetically and chemically, by

shortening the time span through drugs. "Tomorrow" disappears as a center of relevance.

This infantilism would put a bomb under a baby to turn it into a man, and through a psychedelic drug would try to create a mystical experience which few attain even after a lifetime. S. I. Hayakawa, speaking of this false immediacy, says it is a part of our decadent civilization, "We live in an advertising culture. Rolaids offer us instant relief from indigestion. Clairol offers us instant youth and beauty. The new Mustang makes Casanovas out of Casper Milquetoasts. Is it any wonder that there lurks in many of us a hope that a product can be found that offers instant relief from all spiritual ills—instant insight, instant satori?"

On the contrary, happiness, peace and a normal life come through the Long Pull. No one became a tennis player in a day; nor did a juggler learn his art in a second. The little spark of God that is in a man requires a lot of blood, sweat and tears to fan into a flame. The word "asceticism" is taken from the Greek word *askesis* which means training. Did any hippie ever qualify as a split-end for the Green Bay Packers by taking drugs? It is just as vain to think one becomes a physical athlete artificially, as to believe that one becomes a spiritual athlete by any such lack of training. And above all, the Long Pull demands reciprocity in love. Unconscious love is not love. True mysticism has to indicate a tremendous amount of selflessness to be ready for that transcendental love the erring seek, but never find.

> No lover ever seeks union with his beloved
> But his beloved is also seeking union with him.
> When in *this* heart, the lightning spark of love arises,
> Be sure this love is reciprocated in *that* heart.
> When the love of God arises in thy heart,
> Without doubt God also feels love for thee.

Empty House

ठ✍ Youth finds it easier to dig holes than to fill them.
Protests come easy, because early in life things are either
black or white. Enthusiasm quickly takes sides and madly
searches for banners of protest. For a million cries of
"Down with . . ." one would not hear fifty of "Up
with . . ." What is at stake in this negative mood is the
danger of the empty house. Maybe a house is dirty, the fur-
niture is shabby, the utensils leaky. But after one has
thrown out what one calls "junk," the problem remains:
who is going to occupy it? The untenanted house is often
in greater danger than the tenanted one.

Anyone who has ever seen an automobile abandoned on
the highways around New York City in the morning will
find, if he returns the same route in the evening, that mechanical vultures and technological eagles have descended
upon it and stripped it of everything removable, leaving
only the frame. A house recently was purchased for a poor
family; on the day intervening between the signing of the
contract and the occupancy, all the windows were smashed.
Regardless of how "swept and garnished" the empty house
may be, if it is left unoccupied, as the Lord warned, "seven
other devils worse than the first come to dwell there and
the last state of the man is worse than the first."

All the negative commandments of the "Thou shalt
nots" at their best may root out wickedness, but they do
not put goodness in its place. A passion dethroned is not a
virtue enthroned. Giving up drink is not the cultivation
of the spirit. As Sir John Seeley once wrote, "No virtue is
pure which is not passionate; and no character is safe which

is not enthusiastic." Something must be loved; it is not enough to hate evil.

A physician is often filled with anger for a person whom he healed and who then went back to his vices which led to ill health. Plutarch tells us that when the Roman general Pompey was unable to take a city, he would induce its inhabitants to take in a few sick soldiers; they soon recovered and then let in the whole army which conquered the city.

Much moral training of youth breaks down in not inculcating a greater love. Sailors, according to an ancient story, shipwrecked themselves when they became entranced with the song of the Sirens. Some even nailed themselves to the mast so that they might resist plunging into the sea to join the Sirens. But when the harp with melodious chords was played, so pleased were its listeners that the song of the Sirens no longer appealed.

What good do policemen, and even the rigors of law, do against youths who destroy the very schools which feed them knowledge? They may stop the violence, but to what avail unless a new motivation is present? There must be what Thomas Chalmers has called "the expulsive power of a good affection." The boy who will not clean his nails, comb his hair, wash his hands, will do all these things when he meets Suzy. The love principle drives out the dirt principle.

In the days of stagecoaches, someone riding with the driver noticed that suddenly the coachman took his whip and cracked one of the horses behind the ears. Upon inquiring why he did this, since all the horses seemed to be pulling together nicely, the driver answered, "That horse always shies at that post, so I decided to give him something else to think about." For that particular horse it may have been pain; but for the young, it must be a positive idea, by which evil is overcome with good. When the Spirit of Christ and His love becomes deeply imbedded in a heart, one never seeks revenge even when there is nastiness. As Booker T. Washington once said, "My soul is too glad and too great to become the enemy of any man. I resolved that I would permit no man to narrow and degrade my soul by making me hate him."

Evil for evil is dangerous. It acts as a kind of cannon jeopardizing not only those at which it is aimed, but, in its discharge and recoil, those who fire it.

What youths have to realize is what Rabelais once observed, "Knowledge without conscience is soul destroying." It is no good filling minds with facts if ideals are lacking. Vacant heads are invaded by evil just as vacant houses. Almost every revolution is right in its protests; so also are the negations of youth. But where are the reforms? Where are the positive ideas? Even if colleges and universities fail to satisfy the needs of youth, is the occupation of the buildings the answer? Maybe "seven other devils worse than the first will come to dwell there." The air resounds with battle cries; the soil is strewn with the slain, but what is education doing to form conscience? "Be not overcome by evil, but overcome evil with good."

Youth and Their Contact Lenses

&ebdot; A college student complained that her art teacher would not allow her to draw any real object such as an orange, a sunset or a rose. Art, the teacher insisted, was wholly subjective; everything was to be determined by what the mind believed it to be. I asked her if she paid tuition to the school or to the professor himself. Learning it was the latter, I suggested that instead of paying him twenty dollars a week, which was the "objective" fee, that she pay him twenty cents a week, insisting that her mind determined the value of things. Naturally, the professor was very angry and said, "Leave philosophy out of this."

I wonder if youth are not also having their view of the world distorted not just through teachers, but through their own neglect. Let me illustrate with what is happening to hens. Believe it or not, there is a manufacturer of contact lenses for chickens who turns out nearly two hundred thousand lenses a day for the bipeds that once roamed barnyards.

What is the purpose? To distort reality so they will not see things as they are. The hens can see the food and drink which is immediately before their eyes, but roosters will not see hens and hens will not see roosters at a distance. Furthermore, there will be no scratching the earth and rummaging for food, for this is a waste of time. Nor will there be any fighting for seniority. It has been well established that hens have a hierarchy; they have a pecking order. Hen no. 19 in seniority will peck at no. 18 or no. 17 but not at number one or two. It is too much of a challenge. By distorting the hens' view of the objective world, their owners hope to bring about a profitable increase in egg production.

Who is putting such distorting lenses on youth? What limits them to the present, the immediate? What narrows this vision so they see only their peers? What destroys their vision so that they cannot see the future? Where is life going? How is the morning greeted? A. E. Housman wrote of that indefiniteness about the day ahead:

> Yonder see the morning blink
> The sun is up and up must I
> To wash and dress, and eat and drink
> And look at things and talk and think
> And work, and God knows why.

In the absence of a target for the arrows of daily living, is there something which blinds them to the past? Revolutionary youth must realize that new things are not happening in the world; there are only the same old things happening to new people. There are only new labels attached to old ideas. All their plans for a revolutionary take-over of society were tried in the last forty years by youths who wore red shirts, brown shirts and black shirts. Take off the blinkers. The one course that every youth should take should be history, in order to know that the same mistakes were made in previous generations. Not to know what happened before one was born is to remain a child. It may be all well and good for a hen to break off all connections with the past, but for youth to do so is to inflict themselves with amnesia. The best prophet of the future is the past.

Hens with distorted vision no longer have to scratch for a living. They waste no time and lay more eggs. When everything is handed to a youth, there is danger that he will soon begin to believe that spiritual struggle is not necessary to build character. Only when he improves the development of his moral character does he begin to understand better the evil that is still left in him. But when a youth is declining morally, he understands his own badness less and less. We understand sleep only when we wake up. No drunkard understands drunkenness, but his sober wife does. As C. S. Lewis says, "Good people know about good and evil; bad people do not know about either."

As for the situation of the hens, the moral is: Do not allow anyone to destroy an objective moral order outside your ego, otherwise you will go through life laying eggs.

Hippies and Anti-s

~§ As the sea rolls into shore, each wave has its trough and its crest. Extremes are found at both ends of anything that moves. These troughs and crests need not be bad; in fact they may be very helpful to society. Consider two such movements in history and then look at their modern counterparts.

Throughout Christian history, there have always been anchorites and missionaries. The anchorites were those who fled the world because it was evil; they found quiet nooks, hills or deserts away from the world of business and daily life where they gave themselves over to contemplation and prayer. But they were not anti-social or useless. While they did not seem to benefit society materially, they did, however, benefit it spiritually. Their basic principle was physical separateness; they offered their penances to make up for the excesses of others; their poverty, they believed, would bring down the mercy of God on the affluent. Moses on the mountaintop prayed for his people and even stood between the wrath of God and those whom he was leading out of slavery. Just as clouds gather up moisture from the sea and carry it over mountains so it can fall on arid lands, so these seemingly anti-worldly men were really committed to the relaying of prayers and merits to the spiritually dry.

At the other end of the spectrum were the missionaries. They were not alienated from the world; they were immersed in it. Long before the word "involvement" was used, the great missionary Paul was involved in the academies of Athens, the tentmaking business in Corinth, and the evangelizing of the praetorian guard. In all ages, there have been the footloose who suffered the martyrdom of cutting themselves off from their fatherland, breaking family ties in order to immerse themselves in the culture, the sufferings, the agonies, the starvations and the ignorance of other people. I remember being in a small mission in Africa. One missionary said, "I am leaving tomorrow." I asked him where he was going. He said that he did not know where, nor how long he would be away. He would just go out among the people to help them solve their problems, give them medicines and teach them agriculture.

These ascetics and missionaries were the trough and the crest of the waves of a spiritual culture. Now take away from culture a sense of Divine Judgment and the value of a soul; declare God dead, and turn the Kingdom of God into a secular city, and what is left? You have hippies—the twentieth century anchorites who run away from the world, turn their backs on it, isolate themselves from home and society, not to live a life of penance for the sake of others, but to be monks without God, Jeremiahs without Israel, prodigals without a father's house, an unpenitential society—opposing gurus of the concrete desert.

At the other end are the new missionaries or what might be called the "anti-s." Having lost the Kingdom of God, they do not know what they are for; but they do know what they are against. Like missionaries, they burn with zeal, not to build something up, but to tear something down. Violence is not against themselves, for all their swords are thrust outward. They are revolutionists without a program; Stalinists without Marx; they burn draft cards and will burn income tax forms tomorrow. Their throats cry "down" but they are mute when it comes to saying "up." Their protests sometimes are right, but they have no reforms.

But this is not all bad. A hippie is a St. Francis who refuses to work, and an anti is a Francis Xavier without his cross. Every extreme is close to greatness. The quiet ones who run away from society and the angry ones who reject it really should get together. If Mary Magdalene lost the love of Christ which she found in Simon's house, she would have been a hippie. If Paul ever lost the vision he had on the way to Damascus, he would have been an anti. Hippies are potential anchorites, but they need Love; anti-s are the potential political saviors of our people, but they need Truth. Genius to madness is indeed near allied.

The Indeterminists

৺ঌ Many names have been given to our college graduates now emerging into the world. They have been called the "alienated," the "New Left," the "prophetic minority," the "committed" and the "exaggerated." If it be permitted to add to that litany, the title we would give them would be the "Indeterminists." Never before has any generation faced a future less determinable by its present events. Sir Arthur Eddington and other scientists have described the universe by "indeterminism." From their study of the atom they conclude: If we know where the atom is, we do not know how fast it is going. If we know how fast it is going, we do not know where it is. Something escapes. So with the future, there is a vague, undefined, enigmatic, perplexing feeling about our confrontation with the unborn tomorrow. When a child was born, fathers used to ask, "What will he be?" Mothers questioned, "Will he be happy?" Now they are inquiring, "Will he survive?"

The reason for labeling modern youth "Indeterminists" is that they are undecided as to whom they should lend their ear. Who is right? Was Dostoyevsky right as he made one of his characters reflect, "There are two ages of man: one the ascent from the ape to the death of God; the other

from the death of God to the annihilation of man." Does
the future lie in the hands of the Morticians of Deity on
the one hand, and the Nuclear Men on the other? One who
would dethrone God from the heavens and then unseat
man from God's footstool, the earth?

Shall the Indeterminists believe in the theories of Speng-
ler who thought of civilization in terms of four seasons,
and then placed our present age in the winter of discon-
tent? Or will they accept the view of Sorokin who saw cul-
tures of the past at one time inspired by faith, at another by
reason, and at the present as ruled by the senses in which
man dissolves into a kind of an emotional crumble? Will
they embrace the theories of Toynbee who, in his study of
civilizations, discovered that eighteen out of twenty-one
civilizations which have perished from the beginning of
time until now, have decayed from within? Lincoln never
saw America being conquered from without; he predicted
that its real danger would come from moral collapse. Will
the Indeterminists believe Pius XII who, two years before
the atomic bomb blasted Hiroshima, said that if nuclear
energy were not used for peaceful purposes, it would bring
great harm to those places where used, and eventually to the
planet itself. Or will they opt for the world of Paul VI who
warns that little wars are the preparation for another world
war? Will they accept the beliefs of the Slavophiles of the
nineteenth century who saw Russia becoming very wicked,
and then holy once more, bringing Christianity back again
to the world?

Finally, will the Indeterminists see the world as Commo-
dore M. C. Perry did one hundred fourteen years ago, after
his visit to the Orient?

> It seems to me that the people of America will, in some
> form or other, extend their dominion and their power,
> until they shall have placed the Saxon race upon the
> eastern shores of Asia. I think, too, that eastward and
> southward will Russia, her great rival in future aggran-

dizement, stretch forth her power to the coasts of China and Siam: and there the Saxon and the Cossack will meet. . . . Will it be in friendship? I fear not! The antagonistic exponents of freedom and absolutism must thus meet at last, and then will be fought the mighty battle on which the world will look with breathless interest: on its issue will depend the freedom or the slavery of the world. . . . I think I see in the distance the giants that are growing up for that final and fierce encounter; in the progress of events that battle must sooner or later be fought.

In the face of many prophets, the Indeterminists have hope. One aspect of the atom is under our control while another evades us. So, too, in life there is something uncontrollable, namely, the environment in which life will be spent. The young generation may be likened to passengers on a plane. One group would like to cry, "Stop world, I want to get off"; others would like to see it go faster in order that speed would make them forget they were on a journey; still others would like to be served drinks constantly to forget what is going on outside.

But there is yet another group who will be able to make sense of the journey because they have one idea clearly in mind: "where I came from." One can endure the "how" of anything, so long as he knows the "why." These are the Indeterminists who admit they cannot control the passing scene, but can control the journey and make it meaningful. They will have ever before them the Gospel Truth that the Divine-human encounter is made in the crises of life, even those which are beyond our control. The victory lies ahead through a Resurrection. With Dag Hammarskjöld they repeat, "The road, you shall follow it. The fun, you shall forget it; the cup, you shall empty it. The pain, you shall conceal it; the Truth, you shall be told it. The end, you shall endure it."

Daring to Be a "Square"

ও Education in the United States has ceased to be an intellectual privilege; it has become a social necessity. This has resulted in the assumption that the only kind of learning is book learning, but not all youths are suited for book learning. Many an adolescent does not wish to go to school, certainly not to high school. Society is not caring for these people adequately. There are laws against child labor, but once young people have dropped out of school, it is impossible for them to find any labor at all. There is a gap between the moment when the boy drops out of school, and the point where the economic order takes him in. Would it not be well to establish in this country apprentice villages, such as exist in Austria, for job training? Could not unions with their tremendous capital, and management with their great profits, combine to form apprentice schools to train these people not only for a particular industry, but for crafts and sciences in general? Social workers who are wont to excuse juvenile delinquency, are not wrestling with the problem which is to give them a mission and a purpose, an affirmation of their personality, a sense of belonging to society and of having a meaningful career.

A second remedy is not just mission, but vision. One is reminded of the parable, "Blessed are the clean of heart for they shall see God." There is an intimate relationship between purity and the vision of perfect happiness. Purity prepares for a double vision: one, intellectual; the other, spiritual. Intellectual vision is perfected by keeping biological energies intact until Providence prepares the one who shall receive them. Erotic energy, when kept continent is not wasted, but is transformed. The same energy, for example, that a businessman spends in making money could also make him a saint. The energy of a criminal could help remake society. The biological energy that is treasured goes into the intellect and into the making of character. A negative evidence of this is that the youth who falls into erotic excesses will also fall down in his studies. When all of the honeyed treasures of his body are spent, there is no new intellectual life to show. Of the Knights of the Round Table, Sir Galahad was the one who had the strength of ten because his heart was pure. While all the knights sought to see the Holy Grail, that vision was given to this pure-hearted knight, "For such as thou art is the vision, not for these."

There is also the relationship between purity and faith. The want of faith in the modern world is not due to the fact that men are not given reasons for faith; rather the reason comes from want of proper conduct. The impure may see all—except God, and that is why in the end, they will see nothing. Sin will not cheat a man out of the fragrance of the rose, but it will cheat him out of that sweeter soul-fragrance of the Divine, which is folded in every petal.

After mission and vision, comes non-conformism. It used to be some generations ago that the honest, the monogamous, the pure were on the reservation, while the pornographic, the adulterers and the divorced were off it. Today, it is almost the reverse. That is why a special kind of non-conformism is necessary today—namely, a resistance on the part of the good to the evil tide that would sweep away culture and national security.

Socialists used to hold that economic wealth absorbs the have-nots, so that the rich become richer and the poor become poorer. Today, there is another kind of absorption which is even more dangerous, and that is the quantitative absorbing the qualitative. Daring to be a "square" means that honest and decent youths will not fit in with the beatniks and the chiselers, the sharpshooters and the perverts.

The rotten apple is pleasant to the worm, but not to the palate of a man.

The rebirth of youth will come from youth itself. If the legal profession ever became corrupt, it would not be purified by doctors giving lectures, but by honest lawyers regenerating their profession from within. So it is with youth. Social workers, courts and even the clergy will only be the indirect agents for remaking a delinquent youth. The leaders of youth will find among them a vast army who refuse to worship false gods. From the ranks of these young people will emerge "squares" like Lincoln, Washington and other great Americans.

Impenetrability

&.§ A complaint about lack of communication in our culture is often expressed in the jargon of radio and television: "He tunes me out." Parents say this of their children when a plea is made to "please come in before three in the morning, and sober." Husbands and wives mutually accuse one another of being like flint; psychiatrists bemoan patients who refuse to disclose themselves. Somewhere there is a button which closes a trapdoor, flicks off the message and makes minds as indifferent as they are to exaggerated advertisements on T.V.

Psychologists have worked on this phenomenon. Some have tried to master it with client-centered counseling, others by aiming for transference, or the redirection of feelings and desires toward the one who offers help; others by pleading a sympathetic interest or, using what they call an eductive method of "pulling it out" of the patient. These methods have varying success, but for the most part, they are dependent on the patient's readiness to let down the barriers. Failure to establish rapport in the hard cases may be due to professionalism. Anyone is a professional who is more interested in the case than in the person, the disease more than the patient, and the method more than human dignity. The distraught, harassed or anxious patient very quickly knows how authentic is the sympathy offered. In the case of religion, the professional would be the one who would tell the patient to pray, but would neither pray with him, nor pray for him.

In difficult cases of human relationship, the patient is outside the range of the therapist. The latter may say, "I understand you." But the patient could make the same response as the boy did to his father who, while spanking him, said, "This hurts me more than it does you," replied with "Yes, but not in the same place." Professionalism, whether sociological, religious or psychological, lives in a two-story house. There is a descent during the working day to the misery, ills, poverty and neuroses of the sick, but there is always the upper floor to which the professional retires giving himself immunity. Even the best of mothers seeing her child in pain, wishes that she could take that distress into her own body. But such transference is not possible; a basic impenetrability even deepens the sorrow of the maternal hurt.

Since we are dealing only with difficult cases of human illness and unrelatedness, is there no other answer than the psychological? There is, but it is of an entirely different order—the theological, in which love exposes itself to unlove or anti-love. This even demands exposure to the hate of others for the sake of absorbing it. In the face of evil, one becomes a sponge in which rebellion and hate are sucked up and then pardoned and forgiven.

The *yurodivys,* the "born fools" of Russia, do this. In concentration and labor camps, they take on the beatings which were to be administered to others. They know that others might hate back and thus increase the content of evil in the world. But the "born fools," by forgiving the tyrants, diminish the evil of recrimination. It is easy to love when one is loved in return, but to love when love is unreciprocated—such love could never have survived the evolutionary process.

In the struggle for existence, the first animal who turned the other cheek would have perished. All brotherly, friendly and human affections would have perished in the battle for self. The love which absorbs un-love is not from below, but from above. Just as in a family, where one person accepts the burdens, just as in management, where there is a president whose responsibility must absorb all the problems, just as in a diocese, where there must be one heart which becomes conscious of all the zeal and also all the failures, so there had to be in the universe a Divine Consciousness which would gather to itself all the pain and sin of the universe and still love it enough to atone for it and forgive it.

He who loves the most is the weakest. How helpless a mother is before her infant. Her love makes her jump at every cry; her love makes her a slave to that helpless unloving bundle of flesh and blood. But is not Divine Love weak before the unloving, even weak enough to be nailed to a tree? And, on the other hand, is not he who loves the least the strongest, such as a delinquent boy beating his mother?

Before the impenetrable hearts, a loving heart absorbs and above all forgives, saying, "They know not what they do." Forgiveness puts one inside the momentarily unforgiving; it makes return to that which is good possible, because the evil done is not remembered. Somewhere there has to be One Who sighs at the sight of deafness, Who groans in the face of all bereavement and Who sheds tears at the vision of the sinful. Wherever love is professional or imperfect, one may always "shut it off"; but who will refuse to tune in a love so perfect that it drinks in the hate like wine and then pardons? Even the hardened executioner, so impenetrable in his cruelty, at last cried out: "This is Heaven's Love in the flesh."

"Turning Off"

ৰেড় Thanks to our electronic age, we have a handy expression to describe a reluctance to listen and absorb. Parents and teachers complain that as soon as they begin to talk about anything from cleanliness to morality their children "turn me off." College youths sometimes use the word "irrelevance" to give intellectual justification to rejection of courses which they do not wish to follow, *e.g.* "philosophy is irrelevant."

There is nothing new in this but the expression. The Bible had another name for it: in relation to the Divine it was called "hardening of the heart." It was used to describe the penalty of neglect of a moral order among some of the Israelites in the desert, but particularly to the Pharaoh himself. Hardening is not an open rejection of Divine claims, but a trifling with conscience, until spiritual torpor sets in. Herod Antipas at first revered the preaching of John the Baptist, even when his wife hated him. But time passed, and he so forgot the day of his illumination that he shut John up in prison. Then came the decisive act when the drunken braggart made his foolish boast and stained his hands with John's blood as his heart became hardened.

Turning from Biblical language to psychology, "turning off" has another name: it is "repression"—that tendency to throw down into the subconscious mind impulses, thoughts and motivations that are unpleasant, or which run counter to our present way of life. The subconscious mind then becomes like a wastebasket or an old closet, or even a cellar into which we toss rejected thoughts and impulses to get them out of the way. Any repressed tendency which is thrust into a false oblivion actually continues to weigh on the mind, even though one may be unaware of it. The story is told of a woman who invited J. P. Morgan to tea. Knowing how conscious the wealthy man was of his bulbous nose, she kept saying to herself during the day, "I must say nothing about face or anything which will remind anyone of his nose." But the repressed idea broke forth as she said to Mr. Morgan, "Would you like a nose in your tea?"

Now pass to the most general repression of the last fifty or more years. What was it that Victorian society never mentioned, and rarely wrote about? Sex. The life-giving and love-manifesting quality of the human person was repressed. Along came Freud who took off the lid, opened the cellar door, broke open the closet and away flew all the "birds and bees." Stark eroticism emerged in its naked glory. Kinsey later invaded the bedroom, and a new morality was developed which made anything sexual permissible, provided it was done out of "luv" and made one "feel" good.

But it should be remembered that there is never self-expression without corresponding repression, and vice versa. The free expression of carnality of our day necessarily means the repression of the spiritual. The flesh lusts against the spirit, and the spirit against the flesh. A "sex-is-life" age is also a "God-is-dead" age. Religion, morality, self-discipline and decency have been driven underground into the subconscious in our present era. These ideals are as unpopular now as sex was during the Victorian day. When the young "tune them out," they are actually pushing the spiritual down into the lower depths of their minds. Someday, just as there has been a sex explosion, there will also be a religious explosion.

That is why in these days it is important to keep one's balance. Those who sell short our younger generation are just as immature as those who would sell short the forces of religion. There will come a reaction; what has been suppressed will clamor for satisfaction. Today it is the fashion to poke fun at piety and the upholders of morality and order, but it is only a passing fancy. Pitirim A. Sorokin, the famous sociologist, has demonstrated that all societies revolve through a three-phase cycle: sensuality, disintegration and morality. We are presently on the eve of the third. All of us will live to see the reaction setting in.

The Doubts of Youth

⨾ Doubt is either healthy or unhealthy. Healthy doubt is when one sees weaknesses as well as strength in any position. To love America and to believe in it is not to be unmindful of the moral decline which is going on at the present time, not to be passive about arresting violence. Bigots never have healthy doubts. Those who hate Russians never make a distinction between a people and a political system. Newton had a healthy doubt about there being two different kinds of motion: one for the celestial body which presumably moved in circles; the other for earthly bodies which moved in a linear direction. Thanks to his doubt he discovered one law governing both.

In religion, too, a healthy doubt is one which seeks to analyze and find proofs for a position. Thomas the Apostle doubted that Our Lord rose from the dead. He said that he would not believe until he could put his finger into the Crucified Hand, and his hand into the open Side. The doubt was cured, but the Lord reminded Thomas that he should have taken the testimony of those who already had proofs of the Resurrection. But it must not be thought that doubt refers only to beliefs which are outside us, such as the distance of the moon from the earth. One of the healthiest doubts in the world is to doubt oneself or the great inside truth of what you really are. How wise am I? How learned? Do I allow prejudices to influence my thinking?

This brings us to unhealthy doubt by which we destroy within ourselves the capacity to know truth, particularly religious truth. Faith, particularly in the young, is destroyed in two ways:

1. A youth begins to doubt faith when he develops his mind in secular subjects, but allows religious knowledge to remain at the level it was when he was ten years old. A student who becomes proficient in physics, chemistry and anthropology, but has allowed his theology to remain at the Sunday school mentality, will have two disproportionate lobes in his brain. One side grows to the size of the Empire State Building; the other is the size of a filling station. No wonder when the subject of faith comes up, looking down his nose at it, he dismisses it with a sneer: "Oh, that belief is childish."

2. A youth develops unhealthy doubt about religion through immorality and an emphasis on sensate existence. Excessive reading of romantic and pornographic literature also excites feelings to a point where one unconsciously forms a philosophy of life: "Anything is right if it gives me pleasure." Imagination, which can anticipate the infinite, makes the youth certain that life is a mountain of erotic happiness; but repeated experience turns it into a molehill. I can imagine a castle of ten thousand rooms completely walled with diamonds and emeralds, but I will never see it. Soon this discord between what one dreamed and what actually happens begets scorn and ridicule of everything good. Virtue is denied and inner peace becomes a myth.

An immoral life does not affect the speculative intellect, for an astronomer who is a playboy can be just as good an astronomer as one who is a saint, maybe better if he knows more. But grossness does affect the practical intellect which makes judgments. Necessarily, a youth will construct a philosophy of life to suit the way he lives. A bank robber is not the best teacher of honesty. The youth who boldly claims he no longer accepts the Creed, is nine times out of ten the one who rejected the Commandments. More unhealthy doubts arise from erotic excesses than is generally believed. This is what the Lord meant when He said, "You will not come to Me because your lives are evil, lest they be revealed as evil." There is sound psychology in the Beatitude, "Blessed are the clean of heart for they shall see God." If the window is painted black, the sunlight will not enter. Someone said to Pascal, "I wish I could believe as you do," to which he answered, "If you lived as I do, you would believe as I do."

Unless we act upon the beliefs we already have, no new truths will ever be granted us. A youth has to climb up the first hill of a mountain range before he will see the next horizon. If we do not act on the little we know, even that little will be taken away. Unused muscles become atrophied; unpracticed faith becomes doubt. We learn to walk by walking, we learn to write by writing, we learn to love by loving, we learn to believe by believing, not in some abstraction, but in a Person. That is where the Christian Faith begins—with Christ.

About the Author

_____

⤳ Archbishop Fulton J. Sheen was born in El Paso, Illinois. He was educated in schools, seminaries and universities in Illinois, Minnesota, Washington, D.C., Belgium and Italy. Following graduate studies at Louvain University in Belgium, he taught in England and later at The Catholic University in Washington, D.C. His sermons on the radio program, "The Catholic Hour" brought him into national prominence. In 1952 he launched his first television program, "Life is Worth Living" which attracted an audience estimated in the millions throughout the world. He has lectured extensively at universities in the United States and Europe on a wide variety of topics. As National Director of the World Mission Society for the Propagation of the Faith, he wrote and edited two nationally circulated magazines of the Society, *Mission* and *Worldmission*. In 1966 he was named Bishop of the Diocese of Rochester, New York by Pope Paul VI. When he resigned as Bishop of Rochester in 1969, Pope Paul VI named him Titular Archbishop of Newport (Wales). Archbishop Sheen is the author of more than fifty books and a nationally syndicated newspaper column. Since his resignation from administrative duties he has appeared more frequently on radio and television.